SELF GUIDED MEDITATION FOR ANXIETY

FIND CALM IN A CHAOTIC WORLD TROUGH DAILY MEDITATIONS TO HELP YOURSELF OVERCOME PANIC ATTACKS, TENSIONS, ANGER, STRESS, DEPRESSION AND TO ACHIEVE ANXIETY RELIEF.

Table of Contents

Introduction

Meditation is an easy method to quiet your mind, relax, and to escape the stress of daily life. It does not require advanced techniques to learn. Meditation doesn't even require long hours to master. Quite simply, meditation allows you to calm down, to relax, and to gain insight.

Meditation involves quieting the constant babble of our thoughts. This sounds simple, but it's not. Right now, stop thinking for ten seconds. You'll find yourself thinking about those ten seconds and why you're supposed to stop thinking. It's natural for our minds to question and to analyze. Even when we sleep, our brains are active. Our bodies may be resting, but dreams are proof that our minds are not quiet. Meditation lets the body AND mind relax. When that happens, we gain a peaceful experience of calm and insight.

Some methods of meditation try to trick the mind into becoming quiet. The Zen method asks meditators to ponder an idea that doesn't make sense. The mind tries, tries again, and then stops and is quiet. The Zen question "What is the sound of one hand clapping?" is an example. One hand can't clap, so there is no sound. But if one hand tries to clap, what is produced?

The problem with the Zen technique is our thoughts. We give up pondering the question and begin thinking again. We might think "This was silly;" we might remember the grocery list. And so our quiet mind doesn't last. But there are ways to avoid letting the mind keep thinking. They are simple and can be done at any time you have a few minutes free. Have fun!

Studies have documented the medical benefits of meditation. You can explore these in-depth by searching "Meditation" on the internet. Meditation reduces stress, which contributes to disease, unhappiness, and often leads to alcohol or chemical abuse.

Portions of the brain influence us in different ways. Our advanced abilities, such as art appreciation or math problem solving, are higher functions. But our brains control us physically and affect how we function. Basic core responses, such as fear and anger, are controlled by a primal center, nicknamed the "lizard brain" by psychologists. These emotions trigger a shutdown of more advanced brain functions. That way, our entire attention is channeled into a survival mode. In psychological terminology, when we are faced with danger or stress, we enter a "fight or flight" response. Our minds are not capable of deep reasoning when the brain feels under attack. In its defensive mode, our brain has readied the body for the dangers ahead. In the early days, men might have been attacked by a beast. They had to determine whether to run from the beast or fight it.

These days we rarely react to a stressor by fighting. We also don't run away physically. But our bodies react as though we might. Adrenalin floods our system. It remains, as does our stress, as we experience the reaction. Since we don't need to fight or flee, the adrenalin is not required or used. Our brains don't realize the emergency is over, so the small lizard brain still overrides our higher reasoning. We can't reason away stress as a result, just as we can't tell the mind to be quiet.

But meditation gives us a method to remove the stress and mess of "fight or flight." It helps the mind bypass the issue by working at the deep core to calm us. Once that happens, our higher mental functions return. And if we keep working with meditating, we maintain our healthy state. It won't prevent stress from occurring in our lives. But instead of dwelling on it, we can calm ourselves and can see the issue calmly and holistically. Although we can't change how our brains react to outside events, we can adjust how our bodies handle the situation

It sounds so helpful that it must be difficult, like advanced yoga or tai chi. But there are no movements to practice or postures to assume. All you do is relax and let your mind relax too. Meditation has been around for centuries or even longer, although not always called meditation. It is simple. It works. All you have to do is try it. So now, here's an easy way to do that.

PART ONE: UNDERSTANDING MEDITATION, MINDFULNESS AND ANXIETY

Chapter One: History Of Meditation

Benefits of meditation

Meditation Helps to Reduce Stress

The modern-day lifestyle that we lead is hectic and inadvertently leads to stress and anxiety on some level. Stress has become one of the most common problems that people suffer from these days. You may think that you can put it off or might have resigned yourself to the fact that it is a part of your life. However, stress can lead to a myriad of health problems like high blood pressure, an increase in the risk of cardiovascular disorders, and insomnia, just to name a few. The stress chemical in the body is called cortisol. Your body can usually regulate the levels of cortisol within it, but the more your stress levels, the higher the amount of cortisol secreted. This can cause issues like panic attacks. Cortisol secretion needs to be regulated. All of these issues can, however, be dealt with using the help of meditation. It will help in reducing your stress levels and help you deal with anxiety-inducing issues in a productive manner. Overall, by practicing meditation, you will notice a decline in your stress and anxiety levels.

Meditation Helps Keep Emotions Under Control

Humans are emotional creatures. However, it can be hard for us to control our emotions at times, and this can have dangerous consequences. This is especially true in the present world that we live in. The increased amount of pressure and anxiety you experience can cause a build-up of many negative feelings. If you let emotions like anger build-up, it will only harm you. Not just you, but also those around you. Meditation will help you maintain your calm and stay composed even in the face of adversity. When you are able to stay calm, then it is easier to rationalize your thoughts. Apart from this, it will also help you make better decisions. You must not let your emotions control you, and meditation will help you get a handle on your emotions.

Meditation Increases Serotonin Secretion

You might have heard of serotonin, the "happy hormone." The human body secretes various hormones that have a huge impact on how you think and feel. These chemicals in your body will affect how happy, sad, or angry you are. Serotonin is a chemical that helps people stay happy. Studies show that regular meditation helps in increasing serotonin secretion. This chemical has a positive effect on your mind and body. Low levels of serotonin are observed in people suffering from depression and other mental health issues. So, meditation is one of the most effective means of tackling depression.

Meditation Improves the Ability to Focus

Having the ability to focus better is something everyone aims for in life. However, most people have trouble with this. Being able to focus can help you in so many ways. If you are a student, it will help you study better. If you have specific goals in life, you will be able to focus on those goals and work accordingly. Lack of focus can make you lose track of what you do and lead an undisciplined life. Research shows that those who practice meditation tend to have a better ability to focus on their tasks and perform better than those who don't practice meditation. Different meditation techniques will help you hone your ability to focus and enhance your cognitive skills.

Meditation Increases Creativity

It is also said that meditation can get your creative juices flowing. When you meditate and reduce your stress levels, your brain is allowed to function better, and you can be more creative. This creative ability is often negatively impacted by high-stress levels.

Meditation will help you embrace the good and the bad in your life without harming your happiness or health.

Meditation Increases Empathy and the Ability to Connect

You need to learn how to empathize and connect with others if you want better relationships. Meditation will help you learn compassion and thus act compassionately towards people. People who meditate tend to have an increased capacity for kindness and understanding towards others. You will be able to think of things from others' perspectives and react to situations in a better way. Meditation can enhance this empathetic ability and improve your social interactions.

Meditation Helps Improve Relationships

Do you feel like your relationships with your loved ones could use some extra help? Meditation can help you with this. Meditation helps increase your empathy, and this will help you immensely. It helps to increase your awareness so that you can pick up on cues from those around you. This will help you understand how they are feeling in certain situations. By getting a read on the situation, it will be easier for you to react and respond in the right way. Apart from this, it also helps reduce any chances of misunderstandings cropping up. Once your emotions are stabilized, the chances of letting any negativity through will decrease.

Meditation Enhances Memory

Do you feel like you have become forgetful? There could be many reasons behind this, stress being the main culprit. Regardless of what the cause is, meditation can help improve your memory, if practiced regularly. You will be able to focus on things and become more conscious of your surroundings and your own self. You will also be able to retain information for longer and thus be less forgetful. Meditation can be a great memory-enhancing tool regardless of what you do or what your age is.

Meditation Improves Immunity

Another benefit of meditation is that it is a holistic way of boosting your body's immune system. If you feel like you get sick too often or just want to be healthier, you should try meditation. Various meditation techniques like yoga are known to help in strengthening the immune system. By meditating regularly, you will notice a positive change in your overall immunity.

Meditation Helps You Overcome Addictions

Addictions are a serious affliction that can be really hard to contend with. It requires a lot of self-control and discipline to let go of any type of addiction. This could be smoking, alcoholism, or just about any unhealthy habit that has a negative impact on your health and well-being. It's not just the addictions that affect your physical health. There are other addictions like watching too much pornography, using excessive social media, binge eating, etc. These change your body and mind in many negative ways. There are certain meditation techniques, like Vipassana meditation, which is often used to help addicts overcome powerful addictions. Just meditating will not solve all your problems, but it is a great tool to help you move forward and leave your addictions behind. So, if you or anyone you know suffers from an addiction, trying meditation is a good place to start.

Meditation Benefits Cardiovascular Health

It is actually common sense that meditation is good for the heart. If you observe how regular meditation helps you when you need to relax and how it decreases your tendency to be anxious, at that point, is there any good reason why it shouldn't also help reduce the risk of cardiovascular issues, similar to hypertension?

For a considerable length of time, many assumed that to be the case, yet a couple of specialists appeared to be intrigued enough to research and document the physical outcomes on the heart after meditating. The leading researcher to explore this connection was Herbert Benson from Harvard. His important book, distributed in the mid-1970s, *The Relaxation Response,* raised a lot of discussions inside intellectual circles. Through medical testing, he showed that changes occurred in the body.

At first, other colleagues were skeptical of his discoveries. Nobody had ever genuinely thought that there could be medical advantages related to this meditative training. In any case, his testing withstood the thorough investigation conducted by others. In the last two decades, mainstream researchers picked up progressively genuine enthusiasm for the subject. The research started, yet more explicitly, the *American Heart Association Journal* published an article that reported the ability of meditation to bring down an individual's risk factors that are associated with all types of cardiovascular illness.

The *American Journal of Hypertension* recently also published positive reviews on the medical advantages of meditation. In this research, it was found that a gathering of meditating people viably brought down their blood pressure, contrasted with a second group that didn't meditate. The decrease in blood pressure for these individuals was so apparent, truth be told, that the meditators had the option to reduce their utilization of antihypertensive drugs by about 25 percent. Stress is related to something beyond coronary illness.

Stress can cause disruption in a lot of physiological functions. At the end of the day, when you're worried all the time, it manifests in the form of any number of medical issues. One of the systems you may have noticed this in is through gastrointestinal dysfunctions. It's not "all in your head," it's been extensively recorded that changes in physiology and hormones happen in your body in relation to stress. These cause various stomach issues, as a response to a distressing condition - either acute or chronic.

A few people also experience sleep disorders due to stress. In some of these cases, sleep issues are linked with irritable bowel syndrome. Fortunately, these physical changes can be reduced and eased through consistent meditation practice.

Meditation Aids Weight Loss

It's hard to be your best when you're troubled with weight issues. Sadly, numerous people who are overweight do not have a good self-image and lack a sense of self-worth. Without that, they may believe that their ideal life is far out of their grasp. Meditation can do something amazing here, in two different ways. To begin with, it's not unusual to start eating when you're stressed out.

If you are someone who does this, you realize that what you go after first is generally something salty, sugary or greasy. It's not about your absence of self-restraint - blame the hormonal changes related to too much stress instead. Your body craves this kind of unhealthy food when it is under distress.

A lot of research demonstrates that the physical impact of stress on your body can be greatly diminished through meditation. It starts by diminishing the body's cortisol level, which can then mitigate those obstinate yearnings for food. Maybe meditating doesn't offer that equivalent comfort that you get from the bag of chips, candy, or fries (or even all three). Yet, it can help curb those cravings in any case. This is a part of the process that will allow people to pick up a superior mental self-image, which, then, empowers them to concentrate on seeking the life that they need to lead. Stress is very slippery. It penetrates your entire being. Maybe, however, its most notable impending impacts are on the person's immunity. Consider it. How often have you caught a cold or even the flu following an unpleasant event?

Meditation can definitely help you with this also. People under pressure are known to have decreased amounts of basic white blood cells, which are essential for battling foreign attacking microscopic organisms and infections, which can cause cold, influenza, and other illnesses. Meditation is undoubtedly now seen as a great way to insightfully deal with the stress in your life.

Meditation Helps Manage Headaches

A headache is one of the most common signs that your body is experiencing too much stress. What's more, it's difficult to concentrate on what is important to you when a headache is floating over the majority of your thoughts. It's hard to think, and at the same time, it's hard to use sound judgment, and it's tough to enjoy yourself. Maybe it doesn't come as anything unexpected that meditation is the ideal method to loosen up those muscles and suppress that pain.

In addition to the fact that it works for most people, its positive effects are likewise scientifically confirmed. Even for a brief timeframe, going within yourself as meditation allows you to make changes in your brain waves to another higher state. This is a dimension of awareness that is known to help advance the process of healing. The takeaway here is that through meditation, you can adjust your brain waves. Researchers were once convinced that an individual's brain waves are unchangeable. They trusted that we are brought into the world with specific patterns, and these couldn't be modified, despite our ability to switch between different dimensions of cognizance.

Today, however, it's broadly acknowledged that your brain waves *can* be changed—and meditation is one way in which this can be accomplished. The most recent studies have taken a look at people who have been meditating for over fifteen years. Long-term meditation changes the functioning of the brain, which permits the individuals who meditate to achieve a more elevated amount of mindfulness than the individuals who don't. In any case, nothing is preventing you right now from disposing of that migraine through a ten-or fifteen-minute session of meditation, so why not try it?

As you can see, meditation has a lot of benefits for those who practice it regularly. There are actually more ways in which it helps than just the ones mentioned above. If you genuinely want to experience the benefits of meditation, you need to get started.

How Can I Establish A Good Meditation Practice?

One effective way to consistently practice meditation is to create and plan out a practice that you can follow, according to your needs, your daily schedule, routines, and timing.

The thing about meditation is that you need to be mindful of everything that you experience in your session. With mindful meditation, there is a goal and a purpose. It is to help you be conscious and mindful of everything you do.

Benefits Of Establishing A Meditation Practice

A foundation of your meditation session is important because, in many ways, when you set the stones to your practice, your brain will start moving toward making this practice happen. For example, if you decide to buy a new meditation mat, your mind will be reminded (or you will remember) that you purchased the mat, and you want to know the feeling of sitting on the mat and practicing.

Without a firm foundation, you will not be consistent

It won't be long before whatever you're doing eventually crumbles and falls because there's nothing supporting it. That's just one way of describing how important it is to develop a sound meditation practice right from the very beginning of the process.

It helps you create a habit

But although meditation is something that is beneficial for everyone, not everyone is currently putting it into practice. Some people are not practicing meditation at all. Why? Because it isn't a habit. A lot of us lead very busy lives, so sometimes our plates seem too full to take on anything else. There will always be a reason not to start something, which is why it is entirely up to you to make time for it.

The purpose of establishing a meditation practice is because you want to make meditation a habit, a part of your daily life, and something that you are willing to do every day without even thinking twice or resisting it because you are pressed for time.

It makes your practice ingrained, almost second-nature activity in your life

Meditating will become much like how brushing your teeth or showering, preparing something to eat, and even going on a daily commute to work. Those habits are so deeply ingrained in you that you do them without any effort or a lot of thought put into it.

That is what establishing a meditation practice aims to do for you right now, and it is something you need to establish as a foundation to make your practice consistent.

Here is how you can start establishing a meditation practice for yourself.

- Start small. Start small at first by meditating for short periods of time, maybe 5-10 minutes a day, especially if you're new at it. You can do anything for 5-10 minutes a day with no resistance, and the time will pass before you even know it. When you see how easy that was, it keeps you motivated to keep adding onto that. By creating small, achievable goals, you begin building the habit of making meditation a part of your daily life.

- Use tools to help you. There is an app for just about everything these days, even meditation, so why not make the most of the tools you have to help you establish a successful daily practice? There are several apps, such as Headspace and Calm, which can help you enhance your meditation sessions, with everything from timers to ambient sounds to help set the mood. If it helps make your daily practice more enjoyable, why not? You are more likely to stick to something if you like what you're doing.

- Use YouTube. Guided meditations that you like on YouTube can be a great tool, especially for beginners on this journey. It helps you stay on track and on the right path. Some meditations are given on a daily basis, whereas some are based on your goals, such as Meditation for Focus and Meditation for Sleep. Guided meditations make it much easier for beginners, especially to start getting into the flow of things and helps you progress in the right direction with your meditation sessions, especially when you're doing it alone as a solo practice. It would be good to know that you are heading in the right direction.

- Make space. This is extremely important. Making space in your home or anywhere you feel comfortable is a vital part of your practice. A space that is dedicated solely for your meditation sessions should be a place that is safe and comfortable for you, and preferably quiet. Fill that space with anything you need to make you feel comfortable or something that makes you feel like you want to be there for a while. You can fill it with pillows, cushions, pictures that inspire you, incense or scented candles if it helps, and anything that helps soothe your soul and brings you a sense of calm. That will go a long way toward helping you make meditation a consistency in your life if you have a space that you look forward to spending some time in each day because of the comfort and calm that it envelopes you in.

- Make it a schedule. Okay, so not many people like routine and schedule, but if you are starting in meditation practices, this is essential. Make it a point to pencil it into your calendar or make a note of it on your calendar app on your phone. It can be easy for other things going on during the day to take precedence over your meditation session, which is why you need to purposely make that time just to stop and meditate before the day comes to an end, and you realize you didn't get to spend any time meditating at all.

How to Meditate

Meditation is a great - and logically demonstrated - habit for a solid body and mind. Be that as it may, a few people battle with the time, consistency, center, and system required to get meditation right.

What great many people don't know is, you don't really need to take a seat and close your eyes for a considerable length of time a day - in light of the fact that there are other far less demanding approaches to get your psyche into a thoughtful state, and appreciate the advantages of this ancient practice.

For example:

1. While you walk your dog

As you're strolling Jack, instead of meditating a large number of things you're stalling on, take a stab at giving careful attention to your environment.

Recognize the sounds, the general population, the climate. What do you smell? What would you be able to see? What would you be able to hear out yonder? How does your body feel?

By taking a careful walk, you're discharging endorphins, which enable you to build your joy level, and even diminish stress and live longer.

2. While you make coffee or tea

- Begin your morning with more profound concentration, lucidity, and peace by rehearsing this simple reflective custom.

As you make your tea or coffee, concentrate your attention on your developments.

- Close your eyes and notice the tea, take a taste, enjoy it. Furthermore, as you experience the ritual custom, be deliberately mindful of your breath.

- You can likewise apply this while you cook your most loved supper or heat.

3. While you do the dishes

- Doing dishes or clearing your floor doesn't need to be an errand. Actually, this is the ideal time for you to associate with yourself and feel grounded.

- Concentrate on your breath and your body's sensations.

- On the off chance that you see your mind wandering, take yourself back to mindfulness by thinking about the general population and things throughout your life that fill you with delight and appreciation.

4. While you shower

- Have you at any point asked why your best thoughts tend to come while you're showering?

- "The shower is where we can develop mindfulness. When we get tranquil, when we get still, when we rest, you could state, in mindfulness, our natural drive to see associations that we didn't see the prior minute is unobstructed."

- On the off chance that you need to take it somewhat further, as you shower, you can even envision accomplishing your objectives and the feeling that will wash over you as you do.

5. While you tune in to your main tune

- Practicing mindfulness or meditation can be as straightforward as tuning in to your main song - insofar as you're totally centered around your breathing and the feeling that the song brings out in you.

6. While you ride the transport or sit in your auto

- Sit serenely. Take long and full breaths. Recognize the warm sun stroking your face. Welcome the delightful city lights or scenes. Also, let your mind take you all alone trip.

As you now know, the benefits of meditation can be conveyed into the most ordinary exercises - helping you acknowledge life all the more, inhabit a slower pace, embrace new propensities, and be more joyful.

Practical Advice on meditation

To what extent Should I Meditate?

In the event that you are new to meditation, I suggest beginning gradually. Begin with only 5 minutes every day. Bit by bit increment the time more than half a month. When I began reflecting, five minutes felt like an unfathomable length of time. I now practice for 30 minutes every day, and here and there, I am astonished at how rapidly it passes!

Where Should I Meditate?

Locate a comfortable spot where you can sit. You can sit on the floor (utilizing a pad or pad for help if necessary) or sit upright in a seat, with your feet laying on the floor.

A few people suggest that you shouldn't rest on your back; however, I figure you ought to think in whatever stance works for you (unless resting influences you to fall asleep!)

You can meditate anyplace, yet I like having an extraordinary place in my home for my training. You can take in more about making a meditation space in your home here.

What Do I Do?

The least demanding meditation strategy is to count the breath. I forget about each in-breath and breath with a similar number. So my mind concentrates on "One" (in-breath), "One" (out-breath), "Two" (in-breath), "Two" (out-breath), et cetera. When I hit 10 (which seldom occurs before my mind has wandered!), I begin once again at one. On the off chance that you don't care for counting, you can essentially rehash to yourself "in, out... . in, out... "

At the point when your mind wanders, which it WILL DO (that's what the mind does!) tenderly guide your attention back to your breath. On the off chance that you have to begin once again counting in light of the fact that you don't recollect the latest relevant point of interest, that is fine! The key is to not reprimand or judge yourself for giving your attention a chance to wander. Actually ...

seeing that your psyche has wandered is the general purpose of meditation, you are winding up more mindful of the activities of your mind!

Indeed, even the moderately basic guideline to "take after the breath" can sound somewhat obscure or confounding. A supportive method is to bring your attention where you most notice the vibe of the breath — in the chest and lungs? the nose? the stomach? That is your stay. Each time your mind wanders, return to the physical vibes of relaxing.

At the point when thought emerges, it's anything but difficult to get diverted and tail them and draw in them and explain them and investigate them... . An accommodating practice is just to name the contemplations: "stressing," "arranging," "recollecting." Don't stress over making sense of the exact mark for the kind of thought you're having. Simply "considering" will do, as well!

What's more, if the thoughts don't leave? It's still alright.

I adore that depiction of the training.

How Do I Fit This Into My Day?

The critical thing is to make it a propensity. After numerous long stretches of a reliable practice, it will end up being a vital piece of your day, such as practicing or brushing your teeth!

Changing your habits over some stretch of time really makes new neural systems in your mind, and the training will turn out to be a piece of your day by day schedule.

Knocks along the Road

In any case, Nothing's Happening!

Meditation is about non-judgmental mindfulness. We have not to bring desires into our practice. You may encounter a snapshot of significant understanding amid a meditation session. Or, then again, you may be truly exhausted. You may feel fretful and disturbed. Or, on the other hand, you may feel quiet and relaxed.

Meditation is tied in with grasping whatever is right now. The advantages of meditation — more noteworthy mindfulness and discretion, increased calm and empathy — will rise after some time. In any case, every individual session will be totally unique.

So, in case you're exhausted, simply take note of, "This is the thing that fatigue feels like." If you're content, take note of, "This is the thing that satisfaction feels like."

•Meditating for 10 minutes daily is limitlessly superior to meditating for 70 minutes once per week. Attempt to meditate oftentimes (consistently if conceivable), regardless of the possibility that that just means sitting for a couple of minutes.

•Start little. In the event that you endeavor to meditate for 30 minutes right from the beginning, I can practically ensure that you will get disappointed and disheartened. I prescribe beginning with five minutes, and just increase that time when you're comfortable. Regardless of the possibility that you sit for five minutes, and you find that your mind wanders the entire time, you will, in any case, get unfathomable advantages from meditation.

•Pick a gentle alarm. On the off chance that your clock is uproarious and jolting, reckoning the caution will occupy your attention amid meditation.

•Meditate in a peaceful place. Having fewer distractions around you will normally enable you to meditate better, and will make your meditation significantly more profitable.

•It's most straightforward to lose your attention amid your out-breath. Your in-breath is exceptionally articulated and simple to focus on, and the vast majority's mind wanders on their out-breaths (me included). These merits remembering.

•Be simple on yourself when your mind wanders. It's anything but difficult to wind up plainly disappointed with yourself when your mind wanders, yet don't. Your meditations will be substantially more gainful when you delicately bring your mind back.

How to Practice Mindfulness Meditation

Unlike other types of meditation, being mindful doesn't require a large time commitment or a space that is quiet and calm for a specific period of time. While these things will certainly help you get into the required mindset at first, eventually, you will find that you can get your mindfulness on while at the gym, doing chores, or even commuting to and from work. Regardless of where you do it, the basics of mindfulness meditation are always the same.

Stick with a specific time

As with any new habit, it is crucial that you create a routine around your mindfulness meditation practices for the best results. Generally speaking, you can expect it to take about 30 days for a new habit to really stick, which means that you will need to commit to going hard for just four weeks before you can expect to start seeing the best results.

Unfortunately, due to its few requirements and low impact nature, it is often quite easy to push off your set mindfulness meditation time for a later than never comes, especially if they are already very busy as it stands. If you find yourself always coming up with an excuse to get out of meditating at the moment, you may find the following piece of advice particularly useful. "Practice mindfulness meditation for fifteen minutes every day unless, of course, you are extremely busy, in which case you should practice for thirty minutes instead." Don't let the outside world intrude on your potential for inner peace, find a time each day that works for you and stick with it no matter what; in a month's time, you will be glad you did.

Find a quiet place

In order to reach a state of mindfulness, you are going to want to find someplace comfortable, and quiet to sit, though not so quiet and comfortable that you are tempted to fall asleep. Then, all you need to do is breathe deeply, in and out.

Breathe

Start by doing your best to calm your mind by taking a few deep breaths and then announce your intentions aloud to make them more tangible. From there, take several more deep breaths and focus on the sensations that your senses are providing you as you do so. Consider how your lungs feel as they expand and the smells this action brings to your attention. If you are sitting, consider the feel of the chair on your skin, the temperature of the room, and the movement of any wind across your skin. Let the sensations flow from one to another, working their way down your body completely.

Continue breathing deeply, but keep your eyes and ears alert and providing you with more information than you previously thought possible. Focus on this information to the exclusion of everything else. You will likely find it difficult to shut out the constant flow of information that is running through your mind relating to things you need to do, regrets over past actions and plans that must be made, but this is completely normal. If you find your focus drifting away from the moment, take note of the mistake and move on. There is nothing to be gained from beating yourself up over it, and you will only take yourself out of the moment even more.

Visualize

Once you have reached a relaxed state, to remove the excess thoughts that are likely running through your head, all you need to do is picture them as a stream of bubbles that are rushing by in front of your eyes. Simply take a step back and let the thoughts flow past you without interacting with them. If one of them catches your attention and draws you into more complex thought, simply disengage and let it go. Don't focus on the fact that you were thinking about it, because that will just draw you out of the moment, simply remain in that state for as long as possible. Eventually, this will help with negative thoughts you experience in the real world as well.

In fact, with enough time and practice, you will likely find that you are able to maintain a mild meditative state even when you are otherwise focused on the world around you. This is known as a state of mindfulness, and it should be the end goal of everyone who is new to the meditative practice. Being mindful means always being connected to a calming and soothing mental state as well as one that is full of joy and peace, which benefits not just yourself but everyone around you.

Ignore those pesky judgments

Mindfulness is not necessarily quieting the mind or finding an eternal state of calmness. The goal here is simple. You want to pay attention to the moment you are in without judging it. When you judge a thought or something you may have done in the past, you likely, tend to dwell on it. That isn't living in the moment and is not conducive to mindful meditation. While this is easier said than done, it is a crucial step to mindful meditation. With practice, it will be easy to achieve. Be mindful of the moment, of your senses and your surroundings.

Take notice of the times you are passing judgment while practicing mindfulness. Make a note of them and move on. It is easy for your mind to get lost in thought. Mindfulness meditation is the art of bringing yourself back to the moment, over and over, as many times as it takes. Don't get discouraged. In the beginning, you will find your mind wanders a lot. Reel it back in and keep moving forward. Even if your mind does happen to wander, and it will, don't be hard on yourself. It happens. Acknowledge whatever thoughts pop up, put them to the side, and get back on track.

Keep it up

When you first start practicing mindfulness meditation, it is very important that you do so under the understanding that you aren't going to see any results from your hard work at first and rather need to commit to the process fully before you can start receiving any rewards. Specifically, you will need to keep in mind that it is natural for your mind to wander freely for a time before you are able to guide it to where it needs to be. To better understand the mindset that you should be striving for, you might find it useful to consider the moment of complete blankness the mind experiences once it has heard a question, but before it can generate an answer.

Tips For Meditation

Now that you have come to the end of this chapter, we will share some more suggestions and tips to allow you to continue with your meditation practice. These are not aimed at making you an expert but just to assist you on the journey. It is not necessary to try all of these tips at the same time. You can try one or two at a time to see if they help you. There will be some that work better than others. Find what's right for you.

Begin Your Practice with 2-Minute Sessions

It may sound like it's pointless to meditate for just two minutes, but trust us when we say it's anything but. It's simple to do this and is the easiest way for a beginner to learn to practice meditation. Just dedicate two minutes of each day to meditation. Continue this for a week. It's easier to follow through with these two minutes than pressuring yourself to sit still for half an hour. Once you get used to these two minutes, you can add more minutes the next week and so on. You will soon see that you easily meditate at least 15 minutes daily after a couple of weeks, and that will be more than enough time for most. So don't worry and don't make excuses about not having time. Everyone has two minutes to meditate.

Practice Your Meditation Every Morning

A lot of people say that they will meditate every day in the beginning, but most of them fail to follow through with this claim. Don't assume that you will always remember or be inclined to do it. Commit yourself to meditate every single morning after you wake up. After you wash up, just set aside a few minutes for this, and you will see how much better your day goes. Early mornings are considered the best time to meditate.

Don't Worry About the Process and Focus on Beginning the Practice

When people start meditating or think about starting it, they often waste a lot of time and energy on worrying about how they should go about it. They waste time in looking up too many methods, finding the perfect mat to sit on, learning chants, etc. All of these are a part of the practice but not the *essence* of it. You need not spend so much time on this and should try to go with the flow. Just find a comfortable place to sit where you won't be disturbed or distracted by anything. Sitting right on the ground is completely fine, and so is sitting on a chair. To begin with, focus less on all this and more on spending two whole minutes just meditating. The stress of these trivial things will hinder your meditation. So try to get more used to meditating itself and worry about all this later.

Pay Attention to How You Feel

Once you begin meditating, you need to try being more attuned to your personal feelings. Pay attention to how you feel and how this practice is affecting your body. Tune in to the thoughts that pass through your mind. Don't focus on them but notice them as they flow past. Be accepting of all the feelings and thoughts that you experience during meditation. Nothing is wrong or right, so don't judge yourself for any of it.

Count as You Breathe

Breathing is an important aspect of meditation. Find the right place to meditate and then close your eyes as you sit comfortably. Start concentrating solely on your breathing. Focus on your breath as you inhale and exhale. Notice how you take in air through your nose and into your lungs. Pay attention as it leaves your body. When you take in a breath, count one. Count two when you breathe out. Continue the counting as you keep breathing and focus on this alone. It will help you focus more.

It Is Okay for Your Thoughts to Wander

The human mind tends to wander a lot, and you need to be more accepting of it as you meditate. You don't have to assume that you are not allowed to think anything when you meditate. This can be impossible to avoid, at least at first. When you meditate, try not to think but be accepting when thoughts come in. When you notice your concentrating wandering off from your meditation to your thoughts, push back your mind slowly. It can be disappointing, and you might feel like you are doing it wrong, but it is all right. Just slowly come back when your mind wanders away.

Be More Accepting

Like we already said, it is natural for thoughts to appear as you meditate. Don't be defensive, and try to push them away all the time. Instead, be more accepting and allow them to come and pass. Take note of these thoughts, and you can focus on them later. But as you meditate, allow them to come and go naturally. Your thoughts are a part of you, and you need to accept and forgive yourself for everything that you are.

Don't Stress About the Method of Meditation

You might be worried that you are meditating the wrong way at first. A lot of people get stressed about this and think it will be ineffective if they don't practice the right method or do it the right way. The truth is, there is no perfect method of meditation. You can try the various methods we have mentioned and use them as guidelines, but ultimately, you need to do what feels best for you.

Your Mind Doesn't Have to be Empty While Meditating

Some people think that meditation means getting rid of all thoughts and clearing the mind completely. However, this is not true and can be almost impossible for most people. It can be possible to clear your mind out sometimes, but for the most part, it's not what is essential for meditation. It's normal to have thoughts, and you don't have to force yourself to push them all out. Just be more accepting of them and let them pass without focusing on them. Work more on your concentration, and you will see that it gets easier to reduce distracting thoughts over time.

Take Some Time to Accept Your Thoughts and Feelings

Having thoughts while meditating is totally normal. When a thought passes through your mind, it is okay to take a moment and pay attention to it. In the beginning, we recommend to just let the thoughts pass and focus more on breathing. But over time, you can try noticing more of your thoughts too. You should avoid focusing on anything negative and try to bring in more positive thoughts. When you notice your thoughts, you will be able to learn more about yourself. But only allow yourself a moment for this before continuing with your meditation.

Learn a Little More About Yourself Every Day

Meditation is not just about improving your focus or being better able to concentrate. It is about helping your mind develop too. When you become more accepting of your thoughts and feelings, you will learn a lot about yourself. Don't push yourself too hard to think or feel a certain way. Be accepting and learn about yourself. No one can know you better than yourself.

Be Your Own Friend

You need to try learning more about yourself, but this should not be done with a mindset of self-analysis and judgment. Instead, be kinder to yourself. Think of it like learning more about someone you *like*. Accept who you are and be your friend. Don't be cruel and judgmental towards yourself.

Pay Attention to Your Body

After you get better at counting breaths and meditating, you can try something else. Now you should try focusing on your body. Do this with one body part at a time. As you meditate, focus on a specific body part and try to pay attention to how it feels. Start with the lowest point in your body and move on until every part of your body has been acknowledged. This will allow you to pay attention to your body and learn more about it. You will be able to notice if something feels wrong too.

Be Truly Determined

You cannot say you will meditate regularly and then fail to follow through. It is important to dedicate yourself to this practice. Don't take it lightly. Make sure you stick to this resolution for at least a few weeks. Motivate yourself to follow through with it every day. It will soon become a habit, but not if you lack determination right from the beginning.

Meditate, Regardless of Where You Are

It doesn't matter if you're on a trip or have to work overtime on some days. Don't skip your meditation practice. You might reduce the amount of time you can dedicate to it, but you should still meditate. You don't necessarily need that meditation corner in your home for this. It can be done while sitting in a car or even while you sit in your office chair.

Use Guided Meditations

It may seem hard to meditate when you first begin. Guided meditations can be instrumental in this case. Use these audio or video files to help you get started. They are very simple and accommodating regardless of whether you are a beginner or have practiced for some time.

Have Someone to Be Accountable To

If you keep by yourself your resolution to meditate, you are less likely to follow through with it. It will be easy to give up because there is no one to berate you over it. This is why you need to have someone that will hold you accountable. It could be a friend or family member. Just keep checking in with them, and they will help you stay on track. You can also find someone to practice it regularly. This could be someone you live with, work with, or even someone who will go to lessons with you. Finding a network of people who are interested in meditation will help in reinforcing your new good habit. These people can help support you through your journey. You can find online forums or communities of people who practice meditation too.

Chapter Two: Anxiety

What is Anxiety?

Anxiety is your body's response to the feeling of fear or uncertainty about what is to come. Some of the symptoms synonymous with fear include:

- Rapid breathing

- Racing heart

- A "burst" of energy

- Butterflies in your stomach

Everyone feels anxious at times; whether it's your first day in school, giving a speech, or going for a job interview, this feeling is quite a regular thing. Anxiety can be a way for our body to keep us safe from harm. For example, imagine you're taking a walk through the forest, and you're dragging your feet because you're tired; however, you see something that looks like a bear or a snake at the corner of your eyes. You will suddenly forget that you're tired and feel a burst of energy that helps you get away from that location.

If you feel anxious about an assignment that is due, anxiety will motivate you and can help you get it done faster than you earlier thoughts. However, when you start feeling anxious about something unusual, then it can be very unhealthy. Unhealthy anxiety is what is known as an anxiety disorder. Any anxiety that impacts on your daily life is a disorder. Rather than have anxiety as a response to danger, the person with a disorder begins to feel anxious in situations that are perfectly normal, like taking a means of public transport or meeting new people.

The Negative Effects of Anxiety

Anxiety increases your heart rate and breathing in the short term; it directs blood flow to your brain where it's needed, and this physical response helps you to face an unwanted situation. However, if it gets too intense, it can make you feel nauseous and lightheaded. If anxiety becomes excessive and persistent, it can have a devastating effect on both your mental and physical health.

You can have an anxiety disorder at any point in your life. The symptoms of anxiety can stay hidden for a while, as such; don't wait till you get the sign before you embrace a lifestyle change, start immediately.

Anxiety disorder will affect your:

Central Nervous System

If you've had long-term anxiety and a series of panic attacks, it will make your brain release stress hormones more regularly than it should. This can increase the occurrence of some symptoms, such as dizziness, headaches, and depression. Some hormones and chemicals in your body are designed to help you cope with anxiety when you feel anxious your brain floods your nervous system with these chemicals and hormones. Examples of these chemicals are cortisol and adrenaline.

Excretory and Digestive systems

This might seem too extreme, but it's true. Anxiety has a way of affecting your excretory and digestive systems. Some of the symptoms you'll notice are diarrhea, stomachaches, nausea, and some other digestive issues. You can also experience loss of appetite occasionally.

Some connection has been noticed to exist between the development of irritable bowel syndrome (IBS) after a bowel infection and anxiety. IBS can lead to constipation, vomiting, or diarrhea.

Immune System

Anxiety triggers your flight or fight stress response, which causes a flow of hormones and chemicals like adrenaline into your body system.

This influx of chemicals will increase your breathing and pulse rate so your brain can get more oxygen. This flow of chemicals and hormones prepares you to react well to an intense situation. It can make your immune system function better for a short while. Your body should come back to normal when you are in a calm environment. However, if you regularly feel anxious or the intense situation lasts for a long time, your body never gets the sign to go back to its original state. If your body does not return to its original state, it can weaken your immune system, thus leaving you vulnerable to all types of infections. Your regular vaccines may also not work well if you have an anxiety disorder.

Respiratory System

Anxiety can make you breathe rapidly and shallowly. If you have been diagnosed with chronic obstructive pulmonary disease (COPD), anxiety can land you in the hospital due to anxiety-related complications. Anxiety can also make symptoms of asthma worse.

A Summary of Causes and treatments

Most people feel anxious at some point in their life, but there can be certain factors or triggers that cause other people to feel it more severely than normal. These can include someone's genetics, their environment, how their brain is wired, and what life experiences they've had. If a person associates something with fear, it is likely they will develop anxiety surrounding that thing. Although it is typical for people to have some sort of trigger for their anxiety, this is not true for all cases. Some people have very generalized anxiety about nothing in particular; they are simply always worried or dreading being out in the world.

For some people, one type of anxiety can cause them to develop another type of anxiety. For example, someone who has anxiety about suffering harm or getting sick might develop a germ-related obsessive-compulsive disorder as a way to ensure they will never get sick. Or, people with a social anxiety disorder might eventually develop agoraphobia if they never force themselves to interact with others.

Risk factors for different types of anxiety disorders typically coexist in people who suffer from them, which demonstrates that no single experience is likely to cause someone to develop a disorder. Scientists have found that nature and nurture are strongly linked when it comes to the likelihood that someone will develop severe anxiety. Genetically, research has shown that people have about a 30 to 67 percent chance of inheriting anxiety from their parents (Carter, n.d.). Although someone's DNA might be a factor in them developing anxiety, it cannot account for all of the reasons that have developed it.

Environmental factors should also be taken into consideration when trying to find the root cause of anxiety. Parenting style can be a large factor in whether or not a person will develop anxiety. If parents are controlling of their children or if they model anxious behaviors, the child might grow up thinking these are normal behaviors they should model. This can lead to feeling anxious based on learned behavior. Other factors, such as continual stress, abuse, or loss of a loved one, can also elicit a severe anxious reaction because a person may not know how to handle the situation they find themselves in.

In addition to the environment, a person's health can often cause anxiety as well. If someone is diagnosed or living with a chronic medical condition or a severe illness, it can cause an anxious reaction. One possibility is if the illness is affecting the person's hormones, which can cause stress, or if their feelings of not having control are worsened by a diagnosis they cannot fix.

Some people might not realize that the choices they make daily could be contributing to their anxiety. Things such as excessive caffeine, tobacco use, and not exercising enough can all cause anxiety. Caffeine and other stimulants can increase a person's heart rate and simulate anxiety symptoms. Not exercising can lower a person's level of happy hormones and make their muscles tense or sore, which can also contribute to stress. A person's personality can also determine how severe their anxiety might be. Shy people who tend to stay away from conversations and interaction might develop more severe social anxiety because they are not exposed to those situations often.

When experiencing anxiety, it can seem like there is no way out, but there are actually quite a few different ways a person can work to ease their worries, ranging from clinical to holistic approaches. What type of treatments will work depends on the person, and often, how severe their struggle is.

A few clinical ways to treat anxiety include counseling, psychotherapy, and medication. These are not the only ways a person can be medically treated, but they tend to be the most conventional routes for treating mental illness. Counseling is a type of therapy where the person is able to talk to a licensed practitioner and receive feedback and advice about their situation and how to handle their emotions. Most counselors have a master's degree in the psychology field and are licensed through their state. This type of therapy is usually considered a short-term solution for people who are struggling but not debilitated by their anxiety.

Psychotherapy is typically a more long-term solution for people whose lives are impacted by their anxiety. This type of therapy can focus on a broader range of issues and triggers, such as a person's anxious patterns or behaviors and how to fix them. Cognitive-behavioral therapy is often used in this type of therapy to work with the person to adjust their thoughts and behaviors.

Some people find relief once prescribed medication to help them manage their anxiety. This route is usually reserved for people who are struggling the most and having trouble calming themselves on their own. There are various types of medications, such as SSRIs (selective serotonin reuptake inhibitors) and SNRIs (serotonin-norepinephrine reuptake inhibitors) that alter brain chemicals to reduce anxiety or worry.

Making changes to their lifestyle and habits can also help people with anxiety relieve some of their symptoms. This is a more natural approach to managing anxiety and can be successful for people who are dedicated to making positive life changes. Small things such as diet adjustments and increasing activity levels can reduce anxious feelings. Establishing a consistent sleep schedule is also important to help someone ensure they are getting enough rest each night. Stress fatigues the body, and it may need more time to fully recuperate at night if it was taxed during the day. Making sure the body has a routine can also make someone feel safe and know what to expect from their day.

Meditation can also be a good way for people to calm their minds and ease anxiety. Taking time during the day to be still and quiet might help someone stop the constant worry they feel during the day and relax for a moment. Once they start training their body to relax, it is more likely that they can keep it up during the day. Finally, avoiding stimulants such as caffeine, sugar, and tobacco, and depressants such as alcohol can greatly improve a person's chances of overcoming their anxiety. These substances contribute to the brain's hyperactivity and can often increase feelings of anxiety.

Getting Rid of Anxiety with Meditation

Meditation instructs us to be progressively aware of the present and less in our minds. We have a propensity for enabling contemplations to enter our psyche and tail them. Occasionally, these are charming considerations, yet commonly these can be stresses, unpleasant musings, on edge emotions, and anxiety.

Frequently, we enable ourselves to pursue these contemplations and even become these considerations. Even though nothing might happen to us physically at that exact second, regardless, we may feel uncertain or on edge about the future because of our reasoning.

Meditation for anxiety is an unmistakable, guided encounter that enables us to work on winding up progressively present, just as furnish a system to manage musings and the truth that is our occupied and dynamic personality. This training is otherwise called care, which once more, prepares our cerebrum to be available by concentrating ceaselessly from intuition and into things that ground us into the present, for example, breathing and physical sensations.

How Anxiety is Reduced with Meditation

Guided meditation for nervousness causes us to watch our contemplations and feelings without decisions. The basic thing the vast majority do when an idea enters their brain is to tail it, judge it, harp on it, and become lost in it. Rather, a standard meditation practice trains us to be available.

This enables us to control the manner in which we see and respond to our nervousness, rather than enabling our uneasiness to control us.

This is supported by studies as well. In fact, Wake Forest Medical Center conducted several of these focusing on brain scans where areas were both deactivated and activated by patients who suffered from anxiety while practicing mindfulness meditation.

It also showed that those volunteers who had no experience with meditation before actually reported relief from anxiety, had their ventromedial prefrontal cortex and anterior cingulate cortex activated. These areas are where both worrying and emotion stem from. Each volunteer had a minimum of 4 sessions that lasted 20 minutes each.

Contemplation for anxiety likewise gives individuals a strategy, instrument to adapt, and arrangement to anxiety and even fits of anxiety as they occur. Frequently, when a fit of anxiety or a wave of anxiety comes, we do not have a clue how to manage it. More often than not, managing it can mean worrying about it, which just serves to intensify the emotions and circumstances. With guided reflection, we have an apparatus that we can go to and use to all the more viably manage anxiety.

Studies have additionally demonstrated that anxiety sufferers who go to guided reflection have revealed expanded sentiments of control, an expanded feeling of general prosperity, just as an expansion in by and large hopefulness. These sentiments go far in alleviating the recurrence and power of anxiety.

Meditating for Anxiety Relief

To see how to think about anxiety, it is in all probability a prevalent idea that you use a guided meditation. This is especially legitimate for sufferers of anxiety; it might be exceptionally redirecting to endeavor to show yourself meditation from a huge amount of headings.

A guided meditation will walk you through the framework, likewise as give suffering proposals to stay focused on the status.

For those of you who want to self-direct your meditations, or in the event that you like to discover what is in store, at that point, I have given a manual for anxiety meditation that will give a well-ordered procedure for moment help.

Well-ordered Guided Meditations for Anxiety

First, locate an agreeable spot. It could be a seat or pad on the floor.

With your eyes open, take a couple of full breaths. In through the nose and out through the mouth.

After 5 or 6 full breaths, tenderly close your eyes.

Begin to see physical sensations and purposes of contact. Notice your legs and back contacting the seat. Notice your feet against the floor. Notice your arms and submits your lap.

Leave your consideration here for about a moment or somewhere in the vicinity.

Bring your consideration now to the breath. Start to see every breath as it passes and the rising and falling impression of every breath.

Maybe you see this ascent and fall on your chest. Possibly, it is your stomach or mouth.

Don't force the breath here; simply watch each in-breath and out-breath as it passes.

As you do this, your breeze may start to meander. You may even catch yourself so somewhere down an idea that you have overlooked that you were notwithstanding attempting to ruminate in any case. When you see your psyche has meandered, just tenderly return your concentration back to the breath.

Notice any suppositions of anxiety or stress that may endeavor to pull your thought away from the breath. As opposed to following these considerations and feelings, essentially observe and watch them. See what happens when you see the tendency. Empower it to pass and reestablish your attentiveness in regard to the breath.

It is significant that you do not pass judgment on these considerations or emotions since judging is losing all sense of direction in intuition. Simply make a delicate note of what the inclination is and come back to the breath. As though you took a plume to the sentiment of anxiety and said "Goodness better believe it, anxiety" and restored your concentration to the breath.

To make the training somewhat simpler, start to consider the breaths they pass. Include every breath and every breath out, up until a check of 10, and afterward begin once again.

If you get occupied or have sentiments of anxiety, begin the check once again, and return your consideration regarding the breath.

Do this for 5 minutes.

Now, enable your psyche to meander. Discharge all emphasis on the breath.

Following a moment, return your consideration regarding the body and the physical purposes of contact.

Delicately open your eyes and notice how you feel.

You have quite recently finished a care meditation for anxiety alleviation.

Here is another incredible guided meditation for anxiety:

This summed up tension loosening up substance material will empower you to happen upon the loosening up response, a freeing from the weight, and a circumstance of physical and scholarly calm through focusing on breathing, taking a gander at the circumstance of your body, releasing up stressing muscles, and pondering to calm your thoughts.

Doing this kind of loosening up will usually help you with inclination normally progressively peaceful, relentlessly free, and higher arranged to rise up to weight.

Uneasiness is the name used to depict the ride of the body's battling or flight response. There are moving degrees of nervousness, from standard focusing and weight... appropriate to out and outfits of uneasiness. We, as a whole, happen upon tension every so often, and this is standard.

Luckily, anxiety can be diminished utilizing unwinding. In addition, stylish loosening up has a securing influence against weight and tension.

Start through getting open to finding a job sorted out or resting where you can release up. Perceive your palms at your sides, and save your legs uncrossed to improve the dissemination framework.

As you initiate this summed up uneasiness extricating up, you have to close your eyes or spotlight your look on one spot in the room.

Taking in a full breath... next discharge the breath out discharging your lungs totally.

Take in a spotless breath, through your nose... by method for and by utilizing detonating the revive by means of your mouth.

Breathe in... What's more, breathe out.

Continue breathing bit by bit this way, completely discharging your lungs with each breath.

Your basic respiratory calms and releases up you... empower your body to discharge up, to get just the ideal degree of oxygen, and to feel quiet. There is nothing you need to do now and no place should you be, besides here, loosening up, getting an expense out of this time for yourself. You merit this time and need this opportunity to work taking care of business. This season of unwinding will enable you to be as quiet and solid as would be prudent. This summed up anxiety unwinding is profitable, sound time. You are taking care of your wellbeing with this summed up anxiety unwinding.

As you keep up on respiratory relentlessly and effectively, direct your consideration toward your body. Notice how you are feeling physically. Without endeavoring to profoundly change anything, essentially, become mindful of the sensations in your body. All you need to do legitimate now in this summed up uneasiness recreation is watched. Be that as it may, you are feeling appropriate presently is alright. None of your real sensations are the reason for concern, albeit some of them might be terrible because of the reality they are indications of developed pressure. Simply word how you are feeling, seeing any indications of stress and nervousness you can likewise have other than attempting to transform anything at the present time.

Range your body, beginning at the best purpose of your head, and moving diving. Direct your consideration toward your head. Watch.

Moving your thought plummeting to the certificate of your eyes, nose, jaw... down to your two shoulders. Seeing every zone, seeing how your body feels. Continue filtering, progressively descending your body. How does your chest area feel? Observe any territories of strain.

Nearing the point of convergence of your body, at the certificate of your stomach. How is this bit of your body feeling? Keep watching your real state. Continue separating your body, moving the point of convergence of your thought downwards.

Touching base at the certificate of your hips... keep watching and moving your thought down. How does this bit of your body feel? Notice any weight, without attempting to change anything profoundly.

Touching base at the level of your knees... how does this region of your constitution feel. Continue checking... legitimate down to your feet.

Delay for a moment in present-day times to watch your entire body, perceiving how your body feels in general. Where is your body the tensest?

Focus enthusiastically on this one spot of pressure... additionally, imagine the solid tissues here giving up their hold, ending up free, getting the opportunity to be loose... discharging the weight. Discharging the strain a little bit at a time, until this region unwinds. Feel the strain unwinding... feel the muscles as they remove, extend... warming and loosening up, as in spite of the fact that they are relaxing into loosening up. Notice the spot your constitution is the loosest. How does the loosening up feel? Imagine this loosening up is warm and tingly, moving... creating... spreading to release up special bits of your body.

Feel your body ending up increasingly loose as the territory of unwinding develops as you proceed with this summed up anxiety unwinding.

Imagine that your breathing is unadulterated and loosening up. Imagine that the oxygen you take in is loosening up, and the carbon dioxide you breathe in out is a strain. The air trade is a master loosening up the structure. Feel the loosening up as you take it in through your nose and relax up your body, adding to the district of loosening up starting at now there. Expel your body's strain, breathing it out by means of your mouth.

Continue exchanging pressure and loosening up. Continue with the summed up tension loosening up exercise.

Feel the easygoing region getting more prominent as you breathe in increasingly more noteworthy loosening up into your body. Breathe in out strain and experience the strain getting more diminutive.

Take in loosening up, and breathe in out strain.

Each breath in gives to the loosening up, a full breath an expanded measure of loosening up is acquainted with your body. Each breath out clears any weight.

Keep taking in loosening up, and respiratory out the weight. Progressively increasingly free with each breath.

(stop)

After a short time, the zones of pressure are close to nothing. Your respiratory can discard them totally. Imagine breath out any last bits of weight.

You are feeling so tranquil... so free... taking in loosening up, and breathing out loosening up.

Take in... Loosen up

Breathe in out... loosen up

Proceed with respiratory effectively and reliably, releasing up increasingly more noteworthy significantly with every single breath.

By and by, as you continue with this summed up nervousness loosening up, check your body afresh, perceiving how your body feels now.

(stop)

Imagine that your body is made of caramel, or chocolate, or some various qualities that can be mollified. As of now, your body looks like a solid, troublesome piece of caramel.

Imagine a conclusion of warmth, opening in your hold close and feet, that begins to placate the caramel that your constitution is made of.

Before protracted, your hands and toes are fragile... getting milder and an expanding amount of liquid. The gleam spreads all by means of your body... from your hands, up to your arms. Feel your palms condensing, progressing. It is an excellent inclination... so loosening up.

Feel the gleam as it continues up from your feet, up to your legs. Notice your legs progressing, just as they are mellowing to a totally released inclination.

Feel the center of your body as the gleam beginning from your palms and legs meets at your stomach. Feel your middle loosening up, melting.

Imagine that your whole constitution is exceptionally delicate... like caramel that has condensed and is inconspicuous and stretchy.

Basically rest, valuing this loosening up. Floating... loosening up.

(delay)

Focus now on your thoughts. Notice your tranquil thoughts. Getting an expense out of this loosening up. Valuing this summed up tension loosening up exercise.

See how you can focus your derivation to a condition of complete calm by thinking about a single word. Ruminate now on "loosen up" by method for reasonably saying, "Loosen up" each time you slowly inhale in, and each time you breathe out a breath out.

Calmly inhale in, "loosen up".

Breathe in out, "loosen up".

Continue breathing, declaring in your mind "loosen up" with every single breath in and yet again with each breath out. Continue with this summed up anxiety loosening up.

(delay)

It is common for your thoughts to wander, and as they do, truly center afresh round "loosen up. "Continue rehashing this word as you appreciate the summed up anxiety unwinding exercise.

(delay)

Concentrate the majority of your consideration on essentially restating, "unwind."

Continue restating this word, seeing how you are totally loose and quiet, floating in a wonderful condition of unwinding.

Presently, just enable your brain to float. You do not have to concentrate on anything by any means. Simply rest and unwind, appreciating this lovely state you are in.

(pause)

Continue unwinding for some time longer, getting a charge out of this charming, quiet inclination. Proceed with the summed up anxiety unwinding exercise. You can loosen up whenever you have to enjoy a reprieve. This assumption of calm that you have right at present can stay with you even after you are totally attentive and alert. You can keep with you the feeling of calm and assurance, and your muscles can remain free. You can feel very as you approach an astounding activity, despite when you experience weight.

Feeling wonderful. Truth be told, whenever you begin to feel on edge, you may significantly realize this tranquil unwinding and find that the anxiety leaves. You may even keep a casual inclination with you as you experience upsetting circumstances. Imagine the stroll in the recreation center and practicality you will enjoy as stressors come at you head-on while yet feeling happy and quiet...

Take a full breath again, filling your lungs totally... likewise, consider to breathe out, exhausting your lungs completely. Continue breathing easily and tranquility.

You can breathe in like this at whatever point, pulling in loosening up, and breathing out the pressure that assembles as the day advanced. Reliably, your breathing can slacken up you, making you strong and adaptable, arranged to adjust to the nerves that come toward you.

(stop)

By and by, the opportunity has arrived to enter this summed up nervousness loosening up exercise. Your essentialness would increment be able to until you are totally attentive, alert, and incredible.

Interruption for a moment to stir your body and ability so you can come back to your mainstream works out.

Rub your palms together, feeling your arms and fingers arousing.

Move your feet all finished, arousing your feet and legs.

Sit attentively for a moment with your eyes open, reorienting yourself to your condition.

Extend in the competition that you need to, empowering your build to mix totally. When you are completely conscious and alert, you can come back to your standard exercises.

Anxiety Could Be The Next Epidemic

Since we realize what guided meditation for anxiety is and how it functions, exactly how terrible and basic is this anxiety thing, in any case?

Well, the uplifting news or terrible news (depending on what you look like at it) is that you are not the only one. Anxiety issue is the most widely recognized type of psychological instability in the US. More than 1 of every 6 individuals being influenced each year.

An anxiety issue can be:

- Obsessive-compulsive disorder (OCD)

- Post-traumatic stress disorder

- Separation anxiety issue

- Phobia issue

- Major burdensome issue

- Social anxiety

- Generalized anxiety issue

- Panic issue

Regardless, anxiety is not always ceaseless or associated with a perplexity. Feelings of anxiety are winding up progressively increasingly common with the systematic stresses and worries of life being amped up in this related and fast-paced world.

News cycles are getting shorter. The proportion of stun and skepticism being pushed out into the world is creating. The amount of hours worked is extending. Bills and expenses are heating up. It is no huge astonishment such an enormous number of people harp on stress and feels the weight from their work, families, and issues.

In fact, on average, a normal person may end up worrying for 55 minutes every day, while people with anxiety disorders may devote over 300 minutes a day anxious.

Anxiety can be feelings of panic and fear. It can cause sleep deprivation. It can even cause physical symptoms such as shortness of breath, nausea, and heart palpitations. Worse yet, your anxiety can cause other illnesses you may have to become significantly worse, including heart disease. Therefore, it is important that even people who don't have a disorder, to work on managing their daily anxiety better.

While this all may paint an evil reality, unbelievably, the anxiety issue is especially treatable. One way, clearly, is through a standard guided meditation for anxiety.

PART TWO: MEDITATION PRACTICES

Chapter Three: How To Calm The Body

Exercise

Exercise is a highly recommended stress reliever for many reasons. Physical activity has many benefits in addition to reducing stress, and these benefits alone (increased health, longevity, and happiness) make exercise a worthwhile habit. And as a stress management technique, it is more effective than others. The combined benefits of these two facts make physical exercise a lifestyle that is worth following.

Do physical activity

The definition of physical activity in this context has not been limited only to exercise. Physical activity is any activity that engages your physique. Mostly it will lead to perspiration. When an individual engages in physical activity, he or she is obliged to concentrate fully on that particular activity. Exercising is a very renowned way to counter depression. Regular exercise has time and again been used as an anti-depressant. When one is exercising, endorphins are boosted. These are chemicals that enable an individual to feel good.

The statistics of how many people deal with stress is always on the upward. When one experiences stress, it has a lasting effect in their lives since it cuts across what an individual is engaging in at a particular time. To eradicate stress completely is an uphill task, and one would rather manage it. Exercising is one of the best methods to manage stress. Many medical practitioners advise that individuals should engage in exercises in a bid to manage stress levels.

The advantages that come with a person engaging in exercises have far been established to be a counter-measure against diseases and as a method of enhancing the body's physical state. Research has it that exercising helps a great deal when decreasing fatigue and enhancing the body's consciousness of the environment. Stress invades the whole of your body, affecting both the body and mind. When this happens, the act of your mind feeling well will be pegged on the act of the body feeling well too. When one is in the act of exercising, the brain produces endorphins that act naturally as pain relievers. They also improve the instances upon which an individual falls asleep. When the body is able to rest, this means that its amounts of anxiety have dropped by a large margin. Production of endorphins can also be triggered by the following practices. They include but are not limited to meditation and breathing deeply. Participation in exercise regularly has proven an overall tension reliever.

Doing relaxation exercises

Another method of reducing stress levels is through the use of some relaxation techniques. A relaxation technique is any procedure that is of aid to an individual when trying to calm down the levels of anxiety. Stress is effectively conquered when the body itself is responding naturally to the stress levels in the body. Relaxation can be often confused with laying on a couch after a hard day. This relaxation is best done in the form of self-meditation, although its effects are not fulfilling on the impact of stress. Most relaxation techniques are done at the convenience of your home with only an app.

The following types of exercise are highly recommended for stress reduction because they have specific properties that are effective in reducing stress in short and long-term stress management:

Yoga

The gentle stretching and balance of yoga may be what people think when they practice, but there are several other aspects of yoga that help reduce stress and to have a healthy life. Yoga entails the same type of diaphragmatic breathing; this is used with meditation. In fact, a few yoga styles include meditation as part of their practice (in fact, most types of yoga can take you to some degree of meditation).

Yoga also includes balance, coordination, stretching, and styles are the exercise of power. All support health and stress reduction. Yoga can be practiced in many ways. Some yoga styles feel like a gentle massage from the inside, while others sweat and hurt you the next day, so there is a yoga school that can work for most people, even for those who have some physical limitations, to be attractive.

Walking

Walking is one of the easiest medications to relieve stress that is excellent because of the benefits this technique offers. The human body was designed to travel long distances, and this activity generally did not cause as much wear as it did. Walking is an exercise that can be easily separated by the speed you use, the weights you carry, the music you listen to, and the location and the company you choose.

This type of exercise can also be easily divided into 10 minutes of sessions, and classes are not needed, and no special equipment is needed beyond a good pair of shoes. (This is an advantage since studies have shown that three 10-minute workouts provide the same benefits as a 30-minute session: great news for those who, due to their busy schedule, need to practice in parts! To find the More smalls!)

Martial Arts

There are many forms of martial arts, and although each one may have little focus, ideology, or set of techniques, they all have benefits to relieve stress. These practices tend to pack both aerobic and strength training, as well as the confidence that comes from physical and self-defense skills.

Generally practiced in groups, martial arts can also offer some of the benefits of social support, as classmates encourage each other and maintain a sense of group interaction. Many martial arts styles provide philosophical views that promote stress management and peaceful life, which you can choose or not accept. However, some styles, especially those with high levels of physical combat, have a higher risk of injury, so martial arts are not for everyone, or at least not all styles work for everyone. If you try several different martial arts programs and talk to your doctor before following the style, you have a better chance of finding a new habit that keeps you fit for decades.

These three examples are not the only types of exercise. They simply show some benefits and are usable by most people. There are many other forms of workout that can be very powerful, such as Pilates, running, weight training, swimming, dancing, and prepared sports.

Everyone brings their stress management benefits to the table, so discover and practice the form of exercise that appeals to you the most.

Mindfulness Body Scan Meditation

This technique requires a more formal atmosphere than the breathing technique as it is best experienced when you are lying down or sitting in a really comfortable posture. While lying down may seem like a fabulous way, initially, it might not be a good idea in the long-run because novices tend to fall asleep in this position. Also, while a good 30-minute duration is needed for effective results, you may make the best use with whatever little time you get.

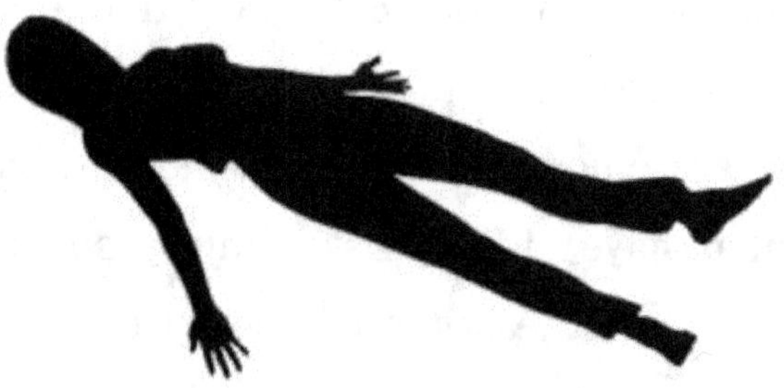

Sit down on a cushion or a chair or lie down comfortably on the floor. Avoid lying on a mattress if you find it difficult to stay awake. Close your eyes because it makes it easy to focus. Now, pay attention to your breath. Slowly move your attention to the places where your body is in contact with your chair or floor. Investigate each section of your body mentally.

The different sensations you experience could be tingling, pressure, tightness, temperature, or anything else. Sometimes, you may not feel any sensation too. Notice the absence of sensations also. Each section of your body becomes an anchor for your mind to hold on so that it doesn't wander away.

Again, be aware when your mind wanders, and gently get it back to where it was before it moved off. When you are done, open your eyes, and mindfully get your focus back on the outside environment.

Another crucial aspect of the body scan mindfulness technique is to release the tension in the various parts of your body as you scan it. When you focus on a particular section of the body, say your shoulders, you suddenly realize that you are holding them too rigid and creating tension in that area. By focusing on that part, tension is automatically released from there.

These are formal ways of body scans and breathing mindfulness meditation techniques. You can do these mindfulness activities even while sitting in your chair in your office. Take a 5-minute break and do a body scan or focus on your breath even as you sit at your desk. You don't even have to get up from your seat. Also, you could do it during your daily commute or while waiting for someone or standing in line for something or anywhere else. Mindfulness meditation does not need anything else but your mind, which is always with you.

Mindfulness Meditation through Mantra Chanting

A mantra is a phrase, word, or syllable that is repeated during the meditation session. Mantras can be repeated in mind, whispered, or chanted aloud. Mantra meditation involves two elements, including the mantra that is being chanted and mindfulness meditation using the mantra as the anchor. Mantra chanting keeps the mind focused and facilitates mindfulness meditation. People also use the mantra as a form of positive affirmations.

Identify the best mantra for your needs. You can choose your mantra based on the reason for the mantra chanting. Are you looking at getting back your health? Are you seeking peace? Do you desire for something to happen in your life? Are you looking for a deep spiritual awakening?

Sit comfortably with your back straight but not rigidly erect. Focus on your breathing first, which will help you get into the mindfulness meditation state. Ensure your intention for the mantra chanting and meditation is clearly imbibed in your mind. Now, start chanting the mantra. Don't expect miracles when you start your chant. Simply repeat the mantra slowly, deliberately, and in a relaxed manner. In this mindfulness meditation technique, mantras are the anchors that help your mind to focus.

There are no 'best' mantras for mindfulness meditation. You can choose anything from the scriptures of your personal religion, or you can choose positive and empowering affirmations such as:

- I am happy and content at this moment.

- All my treasures are inside of me.

- My heart is my best guide.

- It's always now.

- I am complete, and I don't need anything outside of me to make me whole.

- Nothing is permanent.

- This too shall pass.

Breathing Exercises Throughout the Day

Breathing is a fundamental principle of our lives. You must breathe in and out to live. Many times, people suffer from breathing-related problems, which later on affect them. Some have lost their dear lives because of having difficulties in breathing. Others are suffering because they are unable to breathe well. Therefore, it is essential to note the exact significance of breath.

The first important of breathing is that it reduces anxiety. Breathing also helps in the elimination of insomnia. It has the power to manage your day to day cravings, and also it can control and manage your anger response. Breathing brings your whole body into more excellent balance as it can initiate calmness within you. You will realize your entire being becomes normal again after a proper process of breathing and level of stress will be no more. For those having a high level of emotional frustrations can also apply breathing techniques all through the day so that they might get well too. Nothing is as sweet and pleasant as having an excellent relaxed body.

Breathing also aids in other functions within your bodies, such as muscle relaxation, digestion, and even peristalsis processes.

The movement of fluids within your body is made possible by the help of breathing. Breathing helps in the transportation of your body elements such as nutrients and oxygen. It also aids in the removal of waste products. It is better to note that breathing has got that most considerable impact on your respiration as it can donate the required oxygen for respiration. You can acquire the exact energy needed for normal body functions. You will feel strong because power has been formed in your body tissue. Your muscles will be stable since the energy to undertake all your body functions are there. Therefore, you will realize that breathing is a continuous and dynamic process that has no end. Throughout the day, you will understand that breath is an incurring process. Therefore, in this chapter, we are going to look at several breathing ways that can help eliminate and reduce any form of anxiety within you. The main aim of this chapter is to help you with every breathing meditation technique that has the ability and capability to reduce stress ultimately.

The first breathing technique that you will realize is part and parcel of your whole day is reducing stress through **breathing.** Before doing this breathing process, try as much as possible to adopt a good sitting position. The position should be comfortable and relaxing. You can also place your tongue behind your front upper teeth and do the following:

☐   Start by making sure your lungs are empty. You can do this by allowing the air inside to escape through your nose and mouth. You can facilitate this process by doing some enlargement of your shoulder and chest and contracting your stomach so that you increase the exhale process.

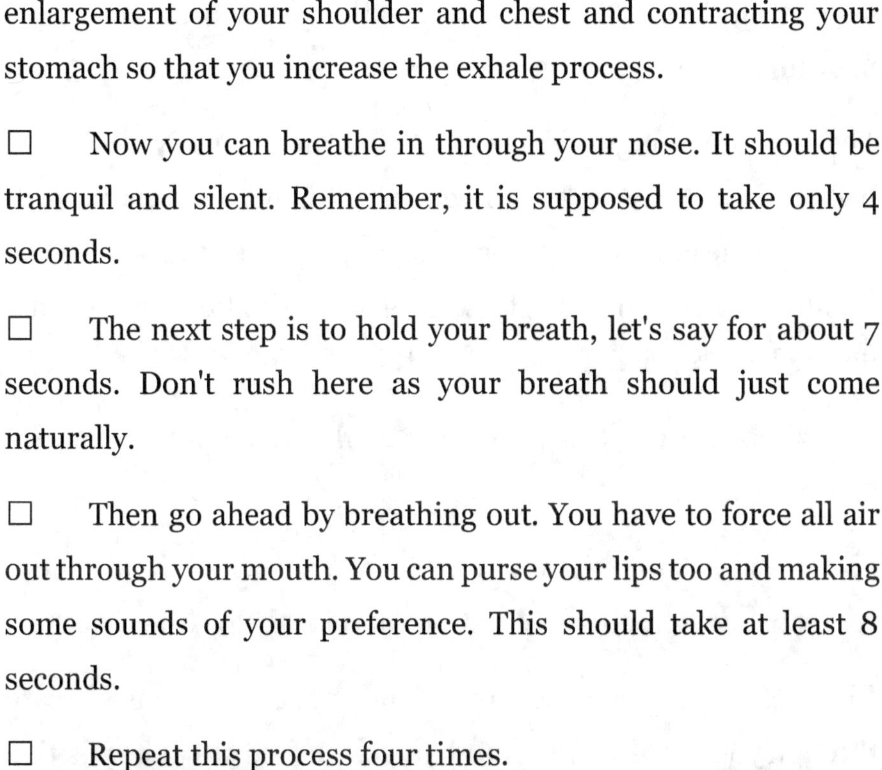

☐   Now you can breathe in through your nose. It should be tranquil and silent. Remember, it is supposed to take only 4 seconds.

☐   The next step is to hold your breath, let's say for about 7 seconds. Don't rush here as your breath should just come naturally.

☐   Then go ahead by breathing out. You have to force all air out through your mouth. You can purse your lips too and making some sounds of your preference. This should take at least 8 seconds.

☐   Repeat this process four times.

Therefore, this breathing technique to delete stress in life is seen as a formidable way to control anxiety. Many researchers, such as Dr. Weil, have recommended these techniques to many patients of anxiety they have healed. According to him, you need to do it in four cycles so that you start realizing its benefits. He went ahead by illustrating that, the moment you do this, feeling of lightheaded encroaches. This will help you to feel relaxed and calm. A relaxed mind and feeling of calmness clear off the stress in your mind. Therefore, your level of anxiety will reduce. You will start having a perfect life without stress and anxiety. Remember, this process takes time. It is now recommended that you perform it in a sitting position that's not only affordable but also comfortable. This type of breathing is the famous 4-7-8 breathing.

The next breathing technique that you can efficiently perform is belly breathing. Belly breathing is not difficult to implement. It is among the most straightforward breathing techniques that can eventually help you to release stress. The following steps are deemed appropriate for your breathing.

☐ Look for a sitting posture or lie flat in any way as far as it is comfortable.

☐ Place your hands on both your belly and chest, respectively. Remember to put one and just below the rib cage.

☐ Now you can start breathing. Take an intense breath through your nose and let your hand be pushed out of its position by the belly. The other hand should not move even an inch.

☐ The next step is to breathe out very loud and produce that whistling sound with your pursed lips. You can feel that palm on your belly moves in as it pushes out the air.

☐ You are allowed to repeat this process more than ten times and make sure to take your time with every single breathing you are undertaking.

☐ Remember to make a note on your feelings at the end of the whole process.

Therefore, belly breathing is a type of breathing that will help you to reduce tension within your stomach tissues. Your chest tissues and even your ribs will feel relaxed. In the end, the anxiety within your body decreases, and your calmness comes back to normal.

We also have roll breathing that you can eventually use to delete some sorts of anxiety, stress, depression, and even unpleasant feeling within you. Roll breathing has several important in your body. Roll breathing enlarges your lungs and, as a result, makes you be able to pay a close watch on your breathing. The rhyming and rhythm of your breath become your full focus. You can undertake this breathing anytime and anywhere. However, as a learner, you should use your back on the ground with your legs bent. Then start by doing the following:

☐ Place your two hands on your belly and chest, respectively. Take a note on the movement of your hands as you concentrate on your breathing process. Continue breathing in and out.

☐ Focus on filling the lower lungs so that your belly moves up when you are inhaling while your chest does not move an inch. It is better to note that breathing in should be through your nose while breathing out must be through your mouth. You are allowed to repeat this process even ten times so that you can realize better results.

☐ After filling and emptying your lungs, you can now perform the other step of filling your upper chest. You can manage this by first inhaling in your lower lungs then increasing the tempo so that it reaches the chest. Here, you should breathe regularly but slowly for quite sometimes. During this process, note the position of your two hands. One placed at the belly will slightly fall as the stomach contract. The one put on your chest will rise as more air is breathed in your chest.

☐   It is now your time to exhale. Go ahead by exhaling slowly through your mouth. You should make that whooshing sound when your hands start falling, respectively. Always, your left hand will have to fall first, followed by your right hand. Still, on this, notice the way tension leaves your body as your mind becomes relaxed and calmed.

☐   Repeat the whole process of breathing in and out for at least 3 to 5 minutes. In this case, make sure you are observing the movement of your chest and belly. Take note of the rolling wave's motion.

☐   Your feeling matters a lot in the whole process. Take a more exceptional look at how you feel in the entire rolling breathing.

Your body regains its full free state, and you will feel more relaxed. You can, therefore, practice this rolling breathing process daily and make sure this goes for several weeks. By doing so, you will be able to perform this kind of breathing exercise everywhere. Also, you can eventually achieve this instantly on most occasions. It will help you regain your relaxation and calmness back. At the end of rolling breathing, your anxiety will be at bay. However, this process is not for everyone since some may feel dizzy during the exercise. You can reduce the breathing speed and accelerate slowly. You can then get up slowly after feeling relaxed, calmed, and lightheaded.

Another breathing technique is **morning breathing**. When you wake up, your body is still exhausted and tired. You feel that your muscles are still weak and wholly tensed. You will realize that your stiffness has got an impact on your day to day activities. The best breathing exercise to follow here is the morning breathing process. It can clear any clogged breathing passages. You can use this method throughout the day to remove the back tension that may be a nagging and a worrying issue to you. The following steps will eventually help you to perform this task with much ease and less effort.

☐　Stand still and then try to bend forward. You should slightly bend your knees, and your hands should closely dangle on the floor or close to it.

☐　Start inhaling and slowly exhaling, followed by a deep breath as you return into a standing position. You can roll upward slowly and making sure that your head comes last from the ground.

☐　Take your time and hold your breath, whether for five seconds or even for 10 seconds. You should do this in your standing position.

☐　Start exhaling. That is, breathing out slowly while trying to make a return to your initial position. You can bend forward a little bit.

☐   Take note of your feelings at the end of the exercise.

The most important thing about this breathing exercise is that it has the power to instill in you more energy, thus enabling you to carry on with every task of the day. You will be relaxed and calm. The level of anxiousness will reduce. In the end, you will feel more lightheaded and entirely energetic.

The next breathing exercise throughout the day can also involve **skull shining breath**. The skull shining breath is also known as kapalabhati in another language where the term initially originated. It is a dominant type of breathing that enables you to acquire a relaxed and calm mind and brain. It always boasts of the right way of killing the anxiety in you by eliminating the tension, especially in your skull. Remember, it is good to note that the pressure of the head can negatively influence your whole day, and the impact can remain with you for long.

Skull shining breath is not difficult to undertake, and this will give you that morale of even performing it throughout the day. You can start by having long breathing in then follow it with a quick and extremely powerful breathing out. Exhaling should originate from your belly, especially the lower part.

However, after getting familiarized with the whole contraction process, you can now start on inhaling and exhaling at a faster rate. Increase your pace here and make sure all the breathing process takes place through the nose. In this process, do not involve your mouth at the initial stages. You can go on with the process repeatedly until you start feeling very much relaxed.

You can now take note of your feelings at the end of the breathing exercise. Remember, this breathing process can eventually prevent muscle tension too. It also helps in releasing abdominal pain. Your worries, stress, anxiety, and even clogged breathing sites will be well.

Breathe Deep

Throughout any day, there are bound to be things that cause your stress levels to rise slightly. There are also going to be thoughts that pop into your head and cause you to feel anxious. Our mind can be our own worst enemy, but the good news is we can take control. There are many ways that we can help ease our fears, and deep breathing is one of them!

These techniques are extremely easy to do and can be done anywhere, even at your desk or on the bus to work! If you find it hard to concentrate, you can also purchase a guided relaxation tape, or download a stress-relieving app, as these will guide you through breathing exercises until you get the hang of doing them yourself.

Try this:

☐   Close your eyes and breathe in through your nose for a count of five, hold it for five, and then exhale through your mouth for five, in a slow and controlled manner. Repeat that for as long as you need to gain control.

☐   Once you're feeling a little calmer or in control, picture the thing that is causing you stress or anxiety as an item or a color. For instance, it might be a black ball, or it might be a gray cloud. It doesn't matter what it is; it simply needs to symbolize the thing that is negatively affecting your day.

☐   Now, visualize yourself forcefully pushing that item far away from you, and visualize it disappearing into the distance.

☐   Finish off with the same breathing technique you started with, before gently coming back into the room.

This is a method you can use for any type of stress or anxiety that is bothering you, and it's a great way to get rid of an issue that is upsetting you at any stage during the day.

Another essential breathing technique is ensuring that we are taking deep, full breaths. When we are even the slightest bit stressed, we start breathing shallowly. These shallow, short breaths do not give us enough oxygen and can even lead to full-blown panic attacks. To stop poor breathing, place your hand an inch or two above your stomach. Now, slowly breathe in through your nose until your stomach touches your hand. Go with our usual 5 counts inhales, and hold for a few seconds before slowly exhaling out through your mouth.

When our breathing is shallow, we only fill up the top portion of our lungs with air. Placing your hand above your stomach ensures that you are breathing deeply enough where your entire lungs are filled!

Deep breathing is the foundation of many calming strategies. It can be done on its own or with other methods like meditation, tai chi yoga, etc. Deep breathing is easy because we need to breathe to remain alive, but strongly and efficiently for mental relaxation and stress reduction. Deep breathing focuses on breathing the stomach thoroughly and clean singly. It is easy to learn that you can do it anywhere, and it regulates your stress levels. Sit down with your back straight, inhale through the nose as the belly grows. Inhale as much clean air as possible into the lungs. It makes it possible to get more oxygen into the blood. Exhale the mouth as the belly drops to force as much air as possible out and close the abdominal tract. If you find it difficult to do this sitting, first try to lie down. You could put your hands on your chest and stomach to see if it's wrong.

Chapter Four: How To Calm The Mind

The world we live in today is a truly beautiful place to be. We may have heard many people say things like "this is a great time to be alive," and they would not be wrong. Limitless opportunities abound around us. Ranging from being able to study to have the careers we have always dreamt of and get our dream jobs to be able to buy the things we want and travel as often as we desire, the world has so much to offer us.

Technology is also a huge part of this mix, as digital communication and social media have made it unnecessary for us to be alone. You can shop online whenever you feel like it, and you can play virtual games and immerse yourself in virtual reality at the click of a button. All these have contributed to making the world a global village that truly runs 24 hours, 7 days a week.

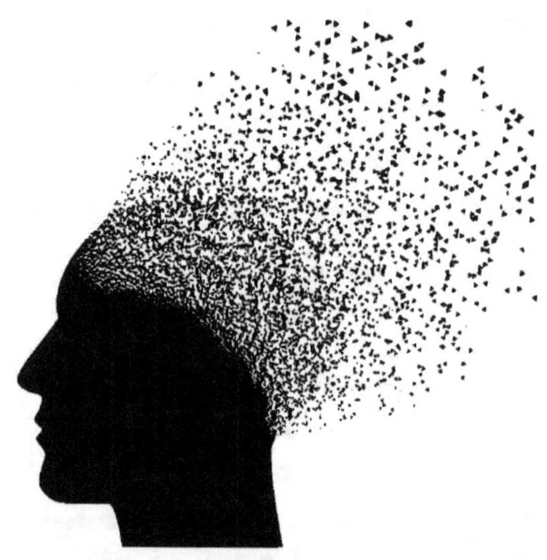

Due to this, we are now expected to spend every part of our days actively working to better our lives. Having some downtime is no longer considered necessary, and in some cases, you could be viewed as lazy for requesting downtime. This is both a good thing and a bad thing.

On the one hand, we are reaping the dividends of how active our society is, on the other hand, we need to consider the toll it is taking on us.

Our brains, just like computers, are not designed to be active all the time. Apart from sleeping at night (which some people do not even take seriously), there is still a lot we can benefit from taking some time to calm our minds and to relax during working hours.

If you are battling with anxiety, you actually need that downtime. You need to unplug from the continuous demands on your time and your mind and calm your mind. Doing this would change and improve the quality of your life.

Visualizing Yourself to Calmness

Visualization refers to the mental formation or representation of an object, image, situation, or set of information. Visualization techniques can also be employed to help with the management of anger. Our brains constantly visualize in the process of simulating future scenarios. This visualization happens so effortlessly that we barely notice it in the same way we barely notice our breathing. When we become aware of our visualization, we can use it as a tool to reduce or reverse anger.

Visualization to help with anger is done by imagining a place or scenario that makes you feel calm or relaxed and focusing on details (sometimes with the aid of audio material such as music) such as smells, sounds, and how good it feels to be in that space. This is usually done when one is sited comfortably and quietly with their eyes closed.

Visualization has four key benefits that improve how we deal with anger. Firstly, it rewires and programs one's brain to help them realize the strategies, tools, and resources they can use to achieve peace and harmony away from anger. Secondly, it builds our intrinsic motivation to take actions necessary to change the habit pattern of the mind, which is reacting to anger. Thirdly, it sparks one's creative subconscious, which helps us with the sublimation of these negative feelings into more socially acceptable forms of expression such as dance, poetry, music, among others. This sublimation helps us express rather than suppress these feelings of anger. Lastly, visualization aids in the law of attraction, thereby drawing you closer to circumstances, resources, tools, and people who can help you achieve your goals of anger management.

Various meditation techniques are also used in anger management and relaxation. Mindfulness meditation and Vipassana meditation both encourage us to accept the anger when it manifests itself and observe it as it is without reacting to it or engaging with it. This usually causes us to be fueled and consumed by it, causing it to become problematic. In retrospect, when we just simply observe anger as an emotion, neither good nor bad, we learn to work with anger, as it is, however or whenever it arises skillfully without it spiraling out of control. When we engage in guided meditation, we learn how to relax and gain relief from stress and stressors that may end up causing anger and allow us to process these feelings healthily. This technique can be used with children too, especially those with heavy temper tantrums. Peaceful and guided meditations help children, adults, and teens improve self-esteem, relieve anxiety and stress, and feel generally refreshed in mind, body, and spirit and develop positive mental attitudes in their daily activities.

Why You Should Calm Your Mind

More clear reasoning

Indeed, it feels great to have the ability to overcome our issues every day. However, at times, the sheer volume of the choices you make can lead to befuddled reasoning and slanted points of view. Clearing the mind of messiness and dispensing with superfluous interruptions will enable you to focus. In a relaxed state, you can settle on better choices, dodge errors, and function with greater mental lucidity.

Setting aside time to calm your mind, using meditation or mindfulness procedures, can assist you with seeing a clearer way through life's difficulties. Unwinding will empower you to place issues in perspective and to prioritize.

Guard your heart

It is presently notable that anxiety can greatly increase your risk of hypertension, cardiovascular failures, and other heart issues. There are researches to show that stress and anxiety can lead to a whole lot of health problems that are heart-related. If you want to live longer and protect your heart, you should make out time to calm your mind.

Drawn out times of stress and anxiety cause hormones to be discharged in the body that influences how the heart functions. This can cause long haul harm if not tended to. Serious anxiety can trigger such a great amount of adrenaline to be discharged that an individual can experience symptoms of a heart attack like palpitations or even have a physical cardiovascular breakdown.

Finding a way to diminish and handle anxiety by figuring out how to calm your mind is vital to taking care of the heart.

Battling ailments

It is common knowledge that people appear to capitulate to more ailments – colds, tummy bugs, coughs, and sore throats – when they feel anxious or exhausted.

Increased stress and anxiety will cause you to succumb to colds, cases of flu, and other infections. This is because your immune system is affected when you are stressed. As such, your immune system cannot really fight infections the way it should.

If you wind up continually fending off infections or you appear to catch every infection that is around you, decreasing your feelings of anxiety could help. Figuring out how to viably calm your mind is critical to decreasing pressure and could empower you to lead a progressively profitable and more beneficial life – which thusly breaks the cycle of stress and anxiety, which adds to your sicknesses.

Fight against depression and anxiety

The World Health Organization estimates that 350 million people all over the world experience the ill effects of depression. Depression and anxiety are presently the leading sources of disability. Specialists in the field feel that it is no happenstance that the rates at which people struggle with depression and anxiety have grown comparatively with their stress levels. These can all be blamed on not taking time to relax and calm your mind.

As well as making your life feel unsavory, uneasiness can genuinely influence your ability to work. Ordinary day by day choices and assignments may feel inconceivable. You may quit taking propane care of yourself and other people under your care, and going to work or even going outside your home might become very difficult for you.

It is important that you protect yourself from these weakening mental conditions, particularly if there is a medical history of either. It is winding up progressively evident that figuring out how to calm your mind is the best technique for mitigating stress and anxiety.

Help with weight loss

A growing number of people are becoming overweight or obese. It is getting increasingly obvious that weight has a direct connection to numerous medical issues, such as diabetes, heart disease, cancer, and strokes. It is crucial to your wellbeing that you can maintain a healthy body weight.

When you cannot calm your mind, your feelings of anxiety grow. Stress causes a hormone called cortisol to be discharged into the circulatory system, and this builds the craving to eat more. This is the reason a considerable lot of people engage in "comfort eating." As well as increase your appetite, it has been indicated that cortisol makes you go after unhealthy foods – foods high in fat and sugar. Foods in this category are considerably bound to make you heap on the pounds.

Setting aside some time to calm your mind can assist you with keeping your body within the healthy weight range for it. Not only will relaxing diminish the measure of comfort eating you take part in, but it will also assist you with seeing the situation with greater lucidity. Lucidity empowers you to design your weight control plans all the more adequately and address your negative dietary patterns.

Calming your mind has numerous advantages – both physical and mental. Your bustling life can make it easy for you to disregard the significance of 'rest' and having the choice to calm your mind. However, it is winding up progressively evident that figuring out how to quiet down and unwind appropriately can help you live a longer and more joyful life. Make it your priority to become familiar with this imperative fundamental ability and set yourself up to receive the numerous rewards.

How To Calm Your Mind Through Meditation

1.Alternate Nostril Breathing

Use your left thumb to hold down your left nostril and breathe in through your right nostril. At that point, close your right nostril with your left forefinger, so both are shut, and hold the breath. Release your left nostril alone and breathe out.

With your right nostril still shut, breathe in through your left. Then close your left nostril with your thumb, so the two nostrils are shut, and hold the breath. Now, take your index finger off your right nostril and breathe out.

This is one set. Complete at least five sets to put the left and right sides of your brain in harmony, quiet your nervous system, and create a sense of calm.

2.The 100-Breaths Method

Close your eyes. Feel your back against your seat, and your feet squeezed immovably on the ground, at that point delicately carry yourself into the present moment. Then start breathing through both nostrils and count as you go on breathing, thinking "and" for each breathes in, and the number for each breathe out— breathe in "and", breathe out "one"; breathe in "and", breathe out "two."

Feel your tummy rude with every inward breath, and let the breaths reduce as you count yourself into a greater feeling of calm. After you arrive at 100, open your eyes, move your fingers and toes, and bow your head in appreciation for the psychological space you created internally.

3.Full Body Breath Sweep

Start by breathing in through your nose, extending your stomach, and counting to five. As you take in a breath, imagine calming warm light filling your feet, and after that, breathe out through your lips at the count of five while envisioning yourself discharging any pressure you may have been holding in there.

Rehash this procedure for your lower legs, your shins, your knees, etc., as far as possible up to your head. After you wrap up your whole body, you'll likely feel lighter, more settled, and calmer.

4.Lip-Touching Breathing

When stirred, your sympathetic nervous system places you in a condition of high alert—that feeling of fight or flight alarm that lets you know there's a type of risk. Your parasympathetic nervous system, when stimulated, produces the contrary inclination—a feeling of relaxation and calmness.

The lips contain parasympathetic nerve strands, making this a basic way to deal with creating a feeling of calm that you can utilize anywhere, whenever. To receive the rewards, you should simply put your lips together, inhale gradually, and say to yourself, "I am calm."

5.Strolling meditation

In spite of the fact that you can do this whenever you're strolling, you might need to locate a serene spot to walk, away from groups, confusion, or noise pollution. If it is a sheltered space, you can walk barefoot. This will give you a feeling of being increasingly connected to the earth.

Remain with your spine straight, with your shoulders and arms lose, and take a couple of inward breaths and exhalations to take in calming energy and inhale out strain.

Then start gradually moving forward and match your breathing with your motion—right foot, breathe in, left foot, breathe out. Utilize the majority of your faculties to completely experience where you are—the warm feeling of sun all over, the delicate sound of wind stirring leaves on trees. The objective isn't to land at a destination; it's basically to be present in the experience of strolling.

6.Meditative bath

It's quite easy to relinquish every other idea when you're standing under a flood of water, set to the ideal temperature for you.

Set aside this time to tune into your faculties. Pick a soap or shower gel you love so that fragrance is intoxicating. Appreciate the feeling of the water on your skin, and feel it dribble down your back, your calves, and your heels.

Notice when you start thinking of the day ahead (or behind you). Try not to pass judgment on the thoughts or yourself for having them. Rather, imagine them going down the drain and afterward take your concentration back to the experience of cleansing your body and mind.

7.Task meditation

Regardless of whether you're vacuuming, cleaning, or washing dishes, it very well may be your meditation time if you immerse yourself totally in action.

Washing dishes, for instance, can be both fulfilling and calming. Feel the warm water on your hands; let yourself appreciate the experience of making something grimy clean once more. Try not to consider completing or what you'll do when you're done. Concentrate exclusively on the doing and check whether you can discover a feeling of acknowledgment and calmness in doing it gradually and well.

8.Mindful Eating

Rather than eating rapidly with one eye on your food and the other on your phone, transform supper time into meditation time. It doesn't take long to eat, so why not set everything aside and set aside this time for yourself? Your mails, messages, and social media pages will still be there when you're done.

Inhale deeply and attempt to recognize the various subtleties of aroma in everything on your plate. At the point when you're eating, take full breaths between each nibble, and consider your meal like a foodie, valuing the various flavors and textures.

If you discover your thoughts meandering to things you've done or need to do, draw your thoughts to the feeling of the fork in your hand. Then inhale deeply, take a bite, and concentrate on relishing the food before you.

Through Mindfulness

Mindfulness transcends meditation. While meditation can be helpful for helping you become more in tune with the workings of your mind, you can reap the benefits of a calm mind through mindfulness.

By simply focusing more on seemingly small details of your life through mindfulness, you can find greater happiness and fulfillment in your life. Better still, you can find that calmness of mind you need to help you deal with anxiety. Below are some ways to calm your mind through mindfulness.

Develop a mindfulness mantra.

Mantras help you remember the important things. They can be useful for mindfulness and calming your mind. A useful mindfulness mantra to help with having a calm mind should be one that reminds you to stay in the moment. It could help if your mindfulness mantra draws your attention to the fact that every day is a new day, and you have the option to start afresh and stay connected with the present moment while separating yourself from the worries in your mind.

Give yourself a reminder that you are not your thoughts.

Whenever a negative thought crosses your mind, simply identify it as merely a thought and move on. Thoughts are like birds; do not allow the ones you do not want to build a nest in your head. Let them keep flying. You are not that feeling of regret or self-doubt; you are not that feeling of anger or scorn. Consciously separate your personality from your thoughts in your mind.

Acknowledge that thoughts emerge normally.

If you cannot change them, then try working to supplant them with other "better" thoughts. Try not to pummel yourself over something you cannot control, but do not overlook them either; basically move past them and decide not to relate to them, even as they cloud your mind.

Relax.

Take a long breath through your nose and exhale it through your mouth. This can calm you and remind you that your thoughts are a little piece of the boundlessly immense world around you.

Thank somebody in any capacity you can.

Indeed, even the little act of saying "thank you" to a waitress or salesperson or receptionist can reconnect you with the present minute, and it can also keep you from getting to be stuck in your own musings, which prevent you from appreciating life as it comes.

Grin at a stranger.

Grinning or smiling helps you concentrate outward to the individuals around you, and by reconnecting with this appreciation for other people, you can connect much better to the present minute and remind yourself just to be.

Take a walk in nature.

Take a walk and blend into the earth around you, and tune in for sounds you would generally have missed.

Leave your telephone on silent throughout the day.

You can also mute your phone's notifications, as these can be diverting and pull you away from the present moment. Your messages will, in any case, be hanging tight for you there later when you are all set to go through them.

Muting your ringer can also prevent every disturbance from obstructing your mind and preventing you from experiencing the genuine feelings of calm you could be having for the duration of the day.

Eat gradually.

Concentrating on the look and the taste of what you eat can help remind you that while all feelings are transient, it is essential to genuinely encounter them properly, as opposed to giving them a chance to pass you by.

Drink tea.

Tea can help quiet your nerves and cleanse your thoughts and connect you more to the present moment.

Wash up.

Showers can assist you with unwinding by compelling you to make a cross over from the clamor of the day, and they can be an incredible method to give your stressors a chance to fall away as they blend into the warmth of the water.

Tune in to instrumental music.

It has been shown to support your capacity to focus, which can raise your strength and quality of your mind and help you calm down when your thoughts would not quit coming.

Handle one of the most stressful things on your plan for the day.

While it is imperative to be mindful irrespective of the demands of your day, do not abstain from finishing a strenuous assignment on your downtime if it is giving you unneeded anxiety.

Have a profound discussion with someone you know.

Completely focus on the other individual and tune in to what they need to say. By not just listening to give your opinion, you can help pull yourself out of your own head and connect all the more profoundly to the moment by demonstrating appreciation to the individuals we converse with.

Watch your preferred show.

It is imperative to take time from your day to reward yourself, and enjoying a comfortable delight like watching a show you like can help you with stepping away from your worries and making the most of your free moments from the clamor of life.

Compose a haiku or any prohibitive poem.

This can move you to be innovative in manners that freestyle composing can't do, and can assist you with recovering a moment in your life that was wonderful yet brief.

Do a word puzzle.

Crosswords can enable your mind to be innovative and can promote your insight, as well as the general clarity of your thought. They can also give you a break from your everyday schedules, all while being fun to finish.

Do the dishes.

Doing the dishes can be an incredible method to take a break from life, and furthermore be profitable while you are taking a break. Washing dishes can assist you with feeling good, and it pulls you away from your present thoughts, which, thus, can give your mind consent to unwind and rest from the pressure of the day.

Look at an art piece you love.

Regardless of whether it is the Mona Lisa, the lyrics of a song you like, or a drawing that your spouse made, nothing is off the table here. Art is emotional, and it can help you to feel and completely immerse yourself at the moment by expressing your appreciation for the works of others.

Play with a pet

Feel the hide underneath your hands and the delicate quality of their skin. Petting an animal can help relieve your stress and connect you to the moment, and can pull you away from your thoughts.

At times it is easy to so busy concentrating on yourself that you neglect to appreciate the world around you. It is easy to get caught in the trap of the mundane and the range of your own objectives, and you neglect to appreciate the excellence of life and the seemingly insignificant details.

Being progressively mindful, as well as meditating, will help you remember every single good thing with time. They would help you realize that there is no sense striving hard and feeling yourself with anxiety and then ending up not enjoying your life. Meditation and mindfulness will help you get away from the struggles of everyday life and remind you to appreciate life again by taking advantage of the beauty of the present moment.

The good part of all this is that everyone has the ability to meditate and be mindful.

Meditation and mindfulness do not need to be tedious or complicated. You can, without much of a stretch, utilize any of these methods during your day to calm your mind and keep yourself focused at the moment and free from your stressors.

Simply remember to stop on occasion and take it all in.

Relaxing the Mind Meditation

One major issue that people struggle with when it comes to sleeping is dealing with insomnia. This is especially true if you allow worrying about keeping your mind and your body awake. It is amazing how much physical anxiety and mental stress can affect your sleep quality. Through meditation, you will learn how to deal with this issue by relaxing your mind and allowing your thoughts to settle down from the day.

Since we are trying to help you fall asleep, do not start this meditation until you are nice and snuggled up in bed. It is up to you what position you want to lie down in. Hopefully, you will fall asleep during or after this meditation, so try to set yourself up for success, Brush your teeth, turn off the lights, set your alarm, and get under the covers. When you are ready to sleep, we can begin.

(PAUSE)

Now that you are settled in bed, gently allow for your mind to get quiet. It has been racing all day long, dealing with responsibilities, tasks, and endless chatter. There is no need to think about anything right now. All you have to do is turn your focus inward and begin to breathe and relax your body. You know exactly how to do this; you have done it many times before. Just focus on your body from the crown of your head to your littlest toes. Breathe and relax. Imagine your relaxation like a big, warm, heavy blanket. It is calming as it wraps around you and feels very comfortable and pleasant. You can let your muscles relax; this is your moment of peace.

(PAUSE)

As you settle into your practice, you may already begin to feel your thoughts drifting away. With each breath you take, allow for your body to sink down into the mattress and fully enjoy this moment. When you fall asleep, any amount of sleep you get is going to be beneficial. There are many different stages of sleep that can be helpful. This is your time to refresh your mind and your body. Use this time to restore yourself and reenergize your body for tomorrow.

(PAUSE)

When you are settling in for sleep, I do not want you to worry about how long you are going to sleep or how much sleep you are going to get. When we try to calculate the hours, we end up just wasting more time. When you set yourself up for success, your body knows exactly how much sleep it needs. Allow for yourself, and you will be waking up rested and alert in no time. You will wake up naturally and peacefully. Just relax, breathe, and settle into this moment with a peaceful mind.

(PAUSE)

Notice now how naturally peace and relaxation are coming to you. Perhaps for the first time all day, you have been able to slow down and just focus on your breath. Allow for this sense of relaxation to carry you to sleep. I want you to imagine these words to be gently carrying you to sleep. You are beginning to float away on a cloud. The cloud is fluffy and soft, like your favorite pillow. Breathe in and release all of your tension; there is no need for it right now. You are drifting further and further...just relax.

(PAUSE)

Before you fall asleep, listen to these affirmations to put you to rest. Just listen softly and allow for my words to pass as you drift off to sleep.

I am feeling very tired.

(PAUSE)

My mind is ready to drift off to sleep.

(PAUSE)

My body is relaxed and ready to sleep.

(PAUSE)

I know how much sleep I need.

(PAUSE)

I am relaxed.

(PAUSE)

I will wake up in the morning feeling fresh and energized.

(PAUSE)

I deserve a full night of sleep.

(PAUSE)

I am falling asleep…

(PAUSE)

Goodnight.

Meditation Time: 20 Minutes

Taming Your Thoughts

If people knew that succeeding in life was dependent on their actions, they would be less likely to worry about their lives. At times, we go through life with regrets and anxiety. We don't feel ready to let go of the feelings that we have embedded within us. Concerning our future, we worry about tomorrow, but a large number of people don't know the power that they have. The power that you have within you can easily become a destructive force or a constructive force that will push you to succeed in life. You have the power to control your life and live it as you wish. What you think about is what you become. If you keep thinking that you will always struggle in life, rest assured that you will struggle to keep things afloat. Conversely, if you truly believe that everything will fall into place and that your time will come for you to enjoy life, expect to live a life full of optimism.

It is important to talk about how you can successfully tame your thoughts to think in the right direction. Without a doubt, there are numerous instances where you will find yourself thinking negatively. How do you control this? How do you prevent yourself from thinking negatively? What are some of the routine changes that you can make to your lifestyle to ascertain that you tame your thoughts? These are some of the questions that this section aims to answer.

Listen to Yourself

Again, this takes us back to the importance of positive self-talk. In order to tame your thoughts, start by listening to yourself. Do this as though you were explaining something to other people. How would you want to tell other people about the story of your life? Without a doubt, you would want to talk about everything that you have done well. No one would want to tell others negative stories about themselves. Therefore, you should adopt a similar attitude when listening to yourself. Focus on treating yourself with the same respect that you would expect from other people. This means that you should strive to focus on thoughts that put yourself in a positive light.

Your Inner Self is Listening

In addition, you should always bear in mind that your inner self is listening to your thoughts; this is the inner you. So, if you continue thinking about negative things, your inner self will listen and conform to how you expect it to behave. When thinking positively, it will also listen to you and adapt to help you perceive life with optimism. Therefore, before blaming other people for the bad things that are happening to you, remember that there is someone within you who is listening to your self-talk.

Befriend Your Emotional Guidance System

There are many cues that you can grasp from your emotions. Learning how to tame your mind can be effectively achieved by being mindful of your emotions. These emotions can easily tell you when you are angry or feeling anxious or overwhelmed about something. Therefore, by being cognizant of your emotions, you can master control over your mind before turning to think about all the negative things.

The point here is that you should pause every time you notice that your emotions have changed. You should take some time to evaluate your emotions and the ensuing thoughts before they gain momentum. The effect of this is that it will help you develop an attitude of thinking twice before doing anything. Before doing anything, you will reflect on whether what you're about to do is positive or not. At the end of the day, you increase the likelihood of making the right decisions without allowing emotions to cloud your judgment.

Find Your Stop Signs

Another practical tip that can make a difference in how you think is visualizing stop signs that signal to you that you should stop thinking about something. Your stop signs will warrant that you can regain your senses and avoid thinking about your past or worrying about your future. The best way of using these stop signs is to remind you that your thoughts are not helping to build you up. For instance, you can come up with a stop sign that reminds you that you are overthinking about events that prevent you from being happy. It might take some time for you to master how to use these stop signs, but the outcome will be rewarding as it will enhance your self-awareness.

Consider Words as Your Nutrition

When thinking about improving our health, we know perfectly well that this can only be done by eating right. The foods that you choose to eat have an impact on your health. In the same manner, the words that float around in your mind have an impact on your mental health. This means that it is essential that you control the information that you feed into your mind. For example, watching horrific content on television might not be as entertaining as you think. In the long run, this will have a negative impact on how you think and the thoughts that frequent your mind.

Remind Yourself with Affirmations

Becoming the master of your own mind also demands that you stay on top of your game. You have to keep yourself engaged in positive gear. Sure, there are instances when you might slip up and think negatively, but with the right affirmations, you will feel unstoppable. Have these affirmations in areas where you can easily see them. Pin them next to your files in your office. Before going to bed, remind yourself of your higher purpose by reading out these affirmations to yourself. They can eliminate anxiety and soothe you to sleep better.

Take Out the Trash

Increasing your self-awareness about your thoughts will give you the advantage of identifying unnecessary thoughts and emotions. When you do this consistently, you will find it easier to declutter your mind. The notion of taking out the trash shouldn't drive you to overthink about your past. Rather, the point here is to develop an attitude where you simply admit that some thoughts are not worth holding on to. Practice meditation exercises as a way of increasing your self-awareness. This is the best way of raising your antennas high enough to pick any signals of unwanted thoughts in your mind.

Pursue Meaning Over Pleasure

Evidently, there is a good reason why you should strive to be happy. Most people have never come to the realization that there are negative effects of focusing too much on striving for positivity. Sure, we all want our lives to be full of happiness. However, we should come to terms with the fact that too much of anything is detrimental. This also applies to happiness. When we go about chasing happiness, we surround ourselves with all the things that can keep us entertained and full of joy. The downside of this kind of life is that it can blind us with unrealistic optimism.

Indeed, without going through pain in life, it is difficult to grow. You will not learn how to deal with the challenges of life that transform you into a strong human being. Therefore, this should signal to you that going through anxiety and stress in the short run is not a bad thing. In fact, it is healthy.

There are two forms of happiness: eudaimonic and hedonic happiness. You should learn to recognize the kind of happiness that you are chasing in your life. Hedonistic happiness is the type of happiness that brings enjoyment and pleasure. Therefore, if you are seeking hedonistic happiness in your life, it means that your main goal in life is to seek pleasure. To these individuals, being happy involves simply doing things they enjoy and seek things that make them feel good.

On the other hand, eudaimonic happiness refers to the type of happiness where happiness is not the main goal in life. In this case, people pursue things of value in their lives that could lead to true happiness. The striking difference in the two forms of happiness is that eudaimonic happiness creates happiness as a by-product of the things that you focus on. Conversely, hedonic happiness only focuses on pleasure as a motivational factor. The beauty behind eudaimonic happiness is that it creates a fulfilling form of happiness in the long haul.

With regard to the notion of taming your thoughts, you should embrace the idea of chasing the eudaimonic form of happiness. Don't just strive to be happy by seeking worldly pleasures. Focus more on what adds value to your life, and you will feel happier in the long run.

Flex Your Muscle Memory

Technology has transformed the way we access information in today's world. The digital devices that we have been introduced to make it easy for us to consume information than ever before. However, this affects our muscle memory since we rely too much on these devices. You can find Millennials struggling with simple calculations where they have to turn to their smartphones. According to a study, to some extent, seniors from the Baby Boomer generation have better memory compared to Millennials.

Consistently sharpening your memory will undeniably help you in many ways. For example, it will ensure that you can hold onto memories that you don't want to forget. We have stressed the importance of letting go of your past. Nevertheless, you should bear in mind that certain memories are worth treasuring, and certain skills are worth practicing. Thus, you should always strive to improve your muscle memory.

From the information detailed in this section, it is clear that taming your thoughts doesn't have to be as difficult as you once thought. It is essential to wake up to the realization that it is equally important to take care of the mind as well as our bodies. Millions of people spend a lot of time, energy, and money to take care of their bodies. People are hitting the gym and ensuring that they eat right to keep themselves fit. But what are they doing to make sure that they are mentally healthy? The mind is not beyond your control. You can train yourself to control your thoughts by sticking to the recommended pointers in this chapter.

Before assuming the significance of taking care of your mind, always keep in mind that your life is based on what you think. So, it is best that you train your mind to think in the direction that you want your life to take. It is amazing to simply know that you have the power to control your life. This power is fueled by the mind. Hence, ensure that you use it wisely.

Chapter Five: Daily Meditation Routines

Morning Affirmations Meditation

Are you looking to start off your day on the right side of the bed? If you want to wake up energetic and ready for any day ahead of you, I highly suggest starting your day off with a morning meditation, topped off with some positive affirmations to get you in a positive mindset.

Of course, you can listen to this meditation at any time of the day, but it is a perfect start to your morning and will only take a small amount of time to energize you and get you started!

As we start this meditation, I now invite you to go ahead and take some deep breaths. With each breath you take, allow the airflow to begin to energize you. Inhale deep into your lungs and exhale everything out.

Breathe in...and exhale. Allow for your breaths to be slow, deep, and calm. Each breath you take brings in the air that your body needs to help get you started. Allow your breaths to fill you with energy and let go of any fatigue you may be feeling at this moment. For the next few moments, this is all I want you to focus on. Just concentrate on your breath. It does not matter what tasks you have for the rest of the day. All you need to think about is breathing in, breathing out, and getting your energy set up for the day.

(PAUSE)

You are going to be ready for this day ahead of you. Breathe in positive energy and allow all positive thoughts to enter your mind. With your next few exhales, let any negative feelings go. If you feel any tension built up in your body, let that go too. You do not have the time nor the energy to waste on negativity. There is only energy and positivity right now. Breathe and remind yourself to be positive.

(PAUSE)

Now, I want you to squeeze your hands into fists gently. As you do this, feel as the muscles strengthen in your arms and your shoulders. Feel now as the strength and energy begin to flow through your veins. You are powerful, and you can accomplish anything you want to. You are capable of accomplishing anything that you need to get done today. You can do anything you put your mind to. Now, relax your fists, and allow your muscles to relax.

(PAUSE)

As your body begins to awaken, feel how warm and energetic you are starting to feel. If you would like, try to open and close your hands a few times. I want you to become mindful of how wonderful your body feels as it wakes up, ready to tackle anything that comes at you today. Allow yourself to become excited for the day, ready for anything that can happen today; there are so many possibilities. Feel now as this positive energy waves through your body and allow your mind and soul to become alive.

(PAUSE)

If you are feeling up to it, I now invite you to enjoy a gentle stretch to get your muscles going. Go ahead and place your fingertips together and gently stretch your arms above your head. Reach for the ceiling and feel the soft pull down your shoulders and into your sides. If you want, gently lean from side to side and feel as your muscles begin to warm up. When you are ready, bring your arms back down and bring your awareness to your toes. Take a deep breath and allow the energy to surge through you.

(PAUSE)

Next, I want you to start to wiggle your feet a little. As you flex your feet, feel as the muscles in your legs enjoy a gentle stretch. Go ahead and spend some time waking your legs up. They are well rested from the night before and are ready to be put to work! Now, hold your feet still and enjoy the sensation of energy tingling through your toes, into your ankles, and up your legs. Take another deep breath in and allow for these sensations to wash over your whole body. The more you move, the more energetic you begin to feel.

(PAUSE)

Now that your body is awake and feeling energetic, it is time to open your mind to positive thoughts to carry you through the day. In the next few moments, we will go over some self-esteem affirmations to boost your confidence and get you excited for the day ahead of you. If, at any point in your day, you feel your stress and anxiety start to take over, I invite you to take a few moments to breathe and repeat the following affirmations to yourself.

As I say the following affirmations, I invite you to continue to focus on your breathing and stretch; however, you feel fit. If you still feel tense in some areas, go ahead and stretch these areas out. This is your time; use it to your advantage. If you start your day off on a positive note, it can get better from there, even if you hit a couple of rocky patches. Feel free to repeat after me or simply listen to the following; it is completely up to you.

I am capable of achieving anything that I work hard for.

(PAUSE)

When times get tough, I have the ability to work through them.

(PAUSE)

I deserve to be happy.

(PAUSE)

I am a strong individual, and I am in charge of my life, even when I cannot control the circumstances.

(PAUSE)

I am worthwhile, even when people make me feel like I am not.

(PAUSE)

I accept myself for who I am.

(PAUSE)

I am proud of all of my hard work and accomplishments.

(PAUSE)

I deserve happiness because I work hard for it.

(PAUSE)

I have many wonderful qualities.

(PAUSE)

I love myself.

(PAUSE)

I am grateful for my life.

(PAUSE)

I am grateful for all of this energy I am feeling.

(PAUSE)

I am ready to tackle this day and anything that comes my way.

(PAUSE)

I will handle everything with as much grace as possible.

(PAUSE)

In tough times, I will remember to breathe and remain calm.

(PAUSE)

I am in control of my thoughts and my body.

(PAUSE)

I choose to be calm and peaceful throughout the day.

(PAUSE)

I am ready to get started with this day and will remember to be at peace.

(PAUSE)

Fantastic. As we draw this meditation to a close, take a few more moments to breathe on your own time and focus your thoughts and intentions for the day. When things become overwhelming, remember to find your breath, and you can work through just about anything. At the end of the day, it all comes down to your mindset, and by starting with this meditation, you are ready to overcome anything with positivity. Now, breathe and get ready to start your day.

(PAUSE)

Meditation Time: 40 Minutes

Breathing Awareness Meditation

Before we begin this meditation, I now invite you to find a position that is comfortable for you. As you settle in, take a few moments to make sure all distractions such as your cellphone and laptop are closed. For the next few minutes, I would like you to just focus on yourself. As you meditate, there is nothing else that matters. If you are feeling anxious right now, that is perfectly okay. We all go through these feelings. What matters right now is that you do something about it.

(PAUSE)

As you settle into position, go ahead and take a nice, deep breath in. If you would like, allow for your eyes to begin to flutter closed. If you are not comfortable with this, simply keep them open and start to soften your gaze. When you are comfortable, all I would like you to do is find your breath. With each breath you take, simply become mindful of how it feels to breathe in fully and exhale everything out. When we feel anxious, we often forget the very basic concept of breathing. Our thoughts begin to move quickly, and our breathing patterns begin to match. Perhaps you are mindful of this, but most likely, you had no idea because you were so focused on being anxious, and that is okay! Just breathe and tune your focus in on yourself.

(PAUSE)

Right now, all you need to focus on is the air entering through your nostrils. It does not matter why you feel anxious, and it does not matter what tasks need to be completed once this meditation is finished. Allow for all of the thoughts in your head to exit and focus only on your breath.

(PAUSE)

On your next breath, I want you to become mindful of how the air travels into your lungs and allow for your belly to expand fully. As you breathe out, feel how your belly gets smaller, and the air moves peacefully back out through your mouth or nose. You may notice that you inhale, feels different from your exhale. Breathe in and feel the comfort of the cool air as it enters your body and how warm it feels as it leaves.

(PAUSE)

If you ever become distracted during your practice, that is perfectly okay. We all get distracted sometimes. If you find yourself getting distracted by noise or thoughts, allow these to pass without judgment and bring your focus back in yourself. There is no need to change anything right now. All you are doing is relaxing and breathing. Simply bring your attention back to your breath and continue a few more moments to breathe on your own.

(PAUSE)

If you would like, you can count with me as you continue to find your breath. On your next breath, I invite you to hold the breath for a few beats. Allow for the air in your lungs to nourish your body and your thoughts. I want each breath to relax you and clear your mind of all worry. When you are ready, we can begin.

Breathe in softly...and hold for one...two...three...and slowly release. Excellent.

Let's do that two more times together.

Breathe in softly...and hold for one...two...three...and release.

(PAUSE)

Breathe in...and hold for one...two...three...and slowly release.

(PAUSE)

Wonderful. At this point, you are probably already feeling much better. Go ahead and take a few more breaths on your own time.

(PAUSE)

During times of anxiety, I want this to be the first practice that pops into your mind. While breathing is a simple task, it can be highly effective. We all experience anxiety in different ways. If you start to become overwhelmed with tasks or emotions, take a step back and find your breath. With each breath you take, gently remind yourself that these feelings will pass, and as long as you are breathing, you are going to be okay. When you are ready, we can continue to the next meditation to keep working through overcoming your anxiety.

Meditation Time: 15 Minutes

The 3 Minutes Breathing Space

This simple exercise is utilized in MBCT programs and Cognitive Behavior Therapies. It helps people get unstuck and move forward with their lives, even after embarrassing breakdowns.

While performing this mindfulness practice, refrain from evaluating and choosing your thoughts. Instead, you have to become aware of them and your breathing. The previous exercises made you concentrate on one part of your body.

Contrastingly, the 3 minutes breathing space will make you expand your senses. As a beginner, you will only be required to focus on your breathing. But you have to be mindful of the effect of respiration on various areas of your body. Feel the sensations it creates and its effects on your body as a whole.

Does that sound too complicated? Well, don't fret because it is very easy to practice. It only involves 3 simple steps.

a)   Firstly, look for a comfortable area wherein you can't be disturbed by anyone. And if possible, turn off your cellphone and laptop. There must be no distractions. Next, notice the thoughts inside your head, and don't change the things you're observing.

b)   The second step involves focusing on your breathing. Sit in a covered flat surface and sit up straight. Once you are settled, concentrate on your intake and expelling of air. Be aware of the rise and fall of your chest and abdomen. Feel the air as it enters and escapes your nostrils. What do you smell? Do you hear your breathing?

c)   Third, you have to expand your senses. You should still focus on your breathing, but all the while, you must be aware of the other sensations your body is feeling. Other noise or disturbances are unnecessary. Are your legs cramping? Do you feel hot or cold? Be aware and focus on those sensations as well.

The goal of this exercise is to establish awareness for body sensations and to emphasize shifting of attention and to move on from one focus to another. Accordingly, you should only linger for a minute in each step. The 3MBS exercise prepares you for other mindfulness practices, and it encourages "moving of attention."

The exercise can help you get unstuck from automatic routines. It also provides you space wherein you can get a breather from stress or taxing tasks.

Mindfulness on the Bus or Train

If you utilize public transportation, you can take the time spent getting where you are going to practice mindfulness meditation as effectively as if you were sequestered peacefully in your own home. There is one caveat; however, in order to practice mindfulness meditation effectively, it is important that you feel comfortable in the space in which you find yourself. If you find yourself in a situation where something requires your full attention, you will likely be unable to reach your full mindfulness meditation potential.

While listening to music while practicing mindfulness meditation in public is not recommended, you may find it helpful to wear headphones as this is a clear signal to those around you that you do not wish to be disturbed. Furthermore, you may find it helpful to set some type of timer because when you get into the zone while being mindful, it can be easy to lose track of time.

With the preliminaries out of the way, the first thing that you are going to want to do is to plant your feet firmly a comfortable distance apart from one another, whether you are standing or sitting. If standing, take care that you are in a place where you can easily keep your balance. With your feet firmly planted, slowly stretch out your body so that you assume the proper posture for your current surroundings. Take a moment to feel your body move with the rhythm of the train/bus and consider how you are connected not just to the transportation you are riding but to all of those who are sharing the journey with you.

Once you feel that you are centered, choose a spot in front of you that is approximately three feet from your current position. Choose a spot that is close to the ground, perhaps just a foot or two above the floor of the bus or train. Slowly lower your eyes to this point on the ground without lowering your neck, it is important to maintain proper posture throughout the exercise. As you feel your eyes begin to dip towards the floor, focus exclusively on all of the sensory information they are providing you. From there, slowly incorporate the sensations that are being provided by the rest of your senses.

In order to tune out all of the noise and movement that naturally comes with riding public transportation, focus on your breathing and concentrate on taking deep rhythmic breaths at a nice slow pace. Once you have found a rhythm that works for you, consider one of the options below as a means of focusing your attention and attaining a state of mindfulness that might not seem possible otherwise. Remember, practicing mindfulness meditation while using public transportation is even trickier to get the hang of than the other types of mindfulness meditation discussed in these pages. Don't get discouraged if you can't clear your mind as easily as you may be able to elsewhere, as with any other skill practice makes perfect.

Ways to focus your attention

1. Depending on the quality of your ride, you may find that the sensation of movement that you are experiencing to be enough to allow you to focus on the moment. Your body will constantly be moving in this situation, providing you with plenty of sensations to focus on. If you have to move around during your trip, consider focusing on the similarities and differences that the two positions provide you. As you breathe deeply, feel the movement coursing beneath your feet, up through your body and all the way to your arms. Use each stop as an opportunity to refocus yourself on

the moment. Don't forget to pay enough attention to your other senses that you lose track of your stop!

2. Depending on the quality of your public transportation, you may find that smell is another great anchor to plant you firmly in the present. This is also great practice for taking in sensations without judging them as you are likely to smell plenty of things that are good as well as bad while utilizing public transportation. Rather than making judgment calls regarding particular smells, simply focus on each unique smell as it appears, without breaking out of the rhythm of your breathing.

3. If the public transportation that you are on is particularly raucous, or if you don't have any other way to keep track of how close you are to your stop, you can count the number of stops remaining and repeat the number over and over again in your mind until it forms a type of mantra. This method of keeping in touch with the moment can also be combined with one of the others for maximum effectiveness.

While on the one hand, practicing mindfulness meditation while surrounded by so many people can present its own unique challenges, on the other hand, it also provides you with a breadth of different sensory information that you are unlikely to get when practicing any other type of mindfulness meditation, including practicing during your commute. Instead of trying to tune everything around you out completely, a more effective choice is to embrace the chaos that surrounds you and use it as a way to drown out any particularly nagging thoughts that have been plaguing you.

Consider the other passengers for example, are they talking to other passengers, ask yourself what they look like, how they act, sound, smell, etc. Each stop provides a host of new ways to focus your attention and thus remain in the moment easier. What's more, you have more sensations to focus on as well. Focus on the temperature changes as you move along your route as that, and any other sensations are likely to change at a moment's notice.

Meditation For Happiness

I want to welcome you to this exercise that will help you cultivate happiness and feel happy.

Find something comfortable to wear.

You can either lie down or sit. You can sit in a chair or sit on the ground with your legs crossed. Let your hands rest in your lap or by your side.

If you feel uncomfortable at any time, you can immediately stop the recording. You simply need to open your eyes, and the meditation ends.

Now, close your eyes and listen to my voice.

Let your mind be free to explore, to smile, and experience happiness.

Concentrate only on your breathing and nothing else.

Your breaths start to become slower and deeper.

Breathe in through your nose and exhale through your mouth. While you breathe in and out, permit yourself to let go of the outside world.

Visualize a path in your mind's eye. The path can be anything, but at the end of the path, you need to visualize a door. This door opens up the path to your inner world.

Push the door open, and you can see bright light all around you. The light feels warm, welcoming, and it helps you relax.

Your inner world is full of bright colors, and it is time for you to step into this wonderful world.

Relax into all the warmth and peace that exists within.

You are the only one that knows this place, and it is your safe haven.

Take a deep breath and shut the door.

Enter this world, immerse yourself in it, and forget all about the external world for a while. This is your personal world of peace and love. You feel safe and happy in here.

This is your time to work on your happiness. Let happiness spread within your body so that it eventually radiates from you.

It is okay even if your mind starts to wander. It is all right, even if you realize that your thoughts have gone off on a tangent.

Remember that you are in charge of your thoughts, and if you feel like your thoughts are wandering, then you can bring awareness back. Listen to the sound of my voice and concentrate only on my voice.

Now, take a deep breath and start to relax your body.

Start with your feet. Will your toes to relax and then your feet.

Feel your legs relax slowly. Now, feel the muscles in your thigh, and then the ones in your abdomen relax.

Gently allow them to relax.

Start to focus on your chest. Focus on the muscles around your ribcage, and let them relax before you move onto your back.

You can now feel the muscles in your shoulders relax. All the tension that you feel disappears.

Now, allow the muscles in your neck to relax and move towards your head.

Take a deep breath and allow your entire body to relax.

Your breath fills up your lungs with oxygen.

Start to slowly exhale until there is no air in your lungs.

Breathe in through your nose for a count of four.

One, two, three, and four.

Hold your breath for a count of two.

One and two.

Exhale through your mouth for a count of eight.

One, two, three, four, five, six, seven, and eight.

Breathe in, hold your breath, and breathe out.

Imagine the path that you took to enter your inner world.

Walk on that path once again, and you are now surrounded by the same bright light that you saw.

Walk on the path that leads you through an evergreen forest. There are pine trees that line the path on either side. The morning sun is shining brightly, and it is casting golden rays of warm sunlight. Continue to walk on this path, and you will find a rock outcropping overlooking a landscape of mountains.

You are surrounded by hundreds of mountain peaks all, and some seem to be closer than the rest. Gaze at this beautiful scenery in front of you and let the feeling of peace wash all over you.

Appreciate the beauty of nature that's all around you and be thankful for it.

Enjoy the view, and give yourself a moment to smile. Take in the beauty that's present before you.

The golden rays of the warm sunlight are illuminating the landscape. The colors are gently mixing with each other all around you, and it looks like a beautiful painting painted by a maestro. Smile and become aware of all that's around you.

Imagine the sounds of birds chirping around you. Enjoy the symphony of the sounds of nature all around you. Take it all in and smile.

Now, you will notice a large tree near you. The tree seems quite old, and it has a large trunk. Visualize this tree in great detail. The bark of the tree looks like that of sweet birch, and its leaves have a sweet smell to them.

A gentle wind is blowing through the forest, and it blows a couple of leaves away from the tree. One such leaf lands in your palm and you smile as the leaf gives off a slight sweet-smelling minty scent.

Smile at the beauty of nature and take a deep breath. Breathe in all the happiness that you feel and breathe out all your worries.

Breathe in and breathe out.

The leaves start to rustle gently all around you. Light and airy sounds surround you.

Everything around you complements one another, and everything seems to be in sync. This synchronization of nature makes you happy and makes you smile.

You are now surrounded by the warm and wonderful sounds.

Listen to the music of nature; you can feel your heart fill up with joy. You are surrounded by beauty, and it makes you feel happy.

Look around; there is a bush with bright green leaves next to the tree. The leaves resemble that of a maple tree, but the bush is filled with small berries like blackberries.

Go ahead and pick a few berries. Now you can eat these tasty-looking berries.

Enjoy the flavors of these berries and savor how wonderful they taste. Start to slowly chew and then swallow these delicious berries.

You can feel the warmth and energy radiate from your core as these berries slide down your throat and into your tummy.

You can feel energy and strength rise within you. This energy spreads from your stomach to your entire body. You can feel this brilliant energy radiating throughout your body. All your senses feel happy.

You feel a sense of relaxation and appreciation wash all over you.

Look at the nature that's present all around you. Take in the warmth of the sunlight, the chirping of the birds, the greenery, and the wonderful scents all around you. Allow yourself to soak up all this goodness and wonder.

This powerful energy continues to course through your body.

It is pure energy that makes you smile.

Bask in this wonderful energy. Let it wash over every cell in your body. Let your body be infused with nature's wonderful energy.

Stay in this place for a couple of moments and smile more.

Now that your body is infused with this wonderful energy, it is time for you to return to reality.

Your inner world has equipped you with all that you need to feel energized and happy when you return to the outer world.

You can visit your inner world whenever you feel low or dull. You can always come back to this inner sanctum of yours and feel good about yourself.

Take a deep breath and bid goodbye to this wonderful place for now. Hold onto the energy that this place gave you. Hold onto the feelings of positivity and happiness.

You feel good about yourself, and you are looking forward to going back to your world.

As you walk, you will notice the door to the outer world. Slowly open the door, take a deep breath, and step inside.

You are now back in the real world, and you are full of happiness and positivity.

Breathe in slowly and deeply.

Take a deep breath through your nose and hold it for a count of four.

One, two, three, and four.

Now, breathe out through your mouth and hold it for the count of eight.

One, two, three, four, five, six, seven, and eight.

Take another deep breath through your nose and exhale through your mouth.

Start to slowly open your eyes and feel the energy of the inner world shine brightly in your body.

Take a deep breath, smile, and return to your day.

You can follow this exercise whenever you want a burst of happiness. It will help you appreciate all that is good in your life and let go of your worries.

Meditation For Heart

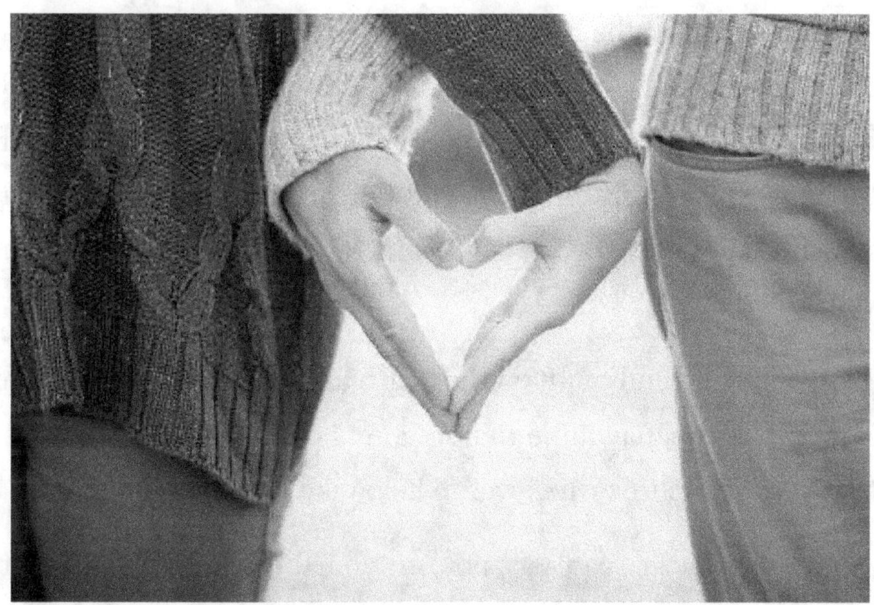

Meditation that comes from the heart and for the heart is important because it can help you lead a life full of wellness, and happiness as well. Here, you'll learn about the best meditation for the heart that is possible, and some important aspects that come from this too.

Why Meditation for Heart?

The heart is a vital part, and it allows you to open up your mind and body in a much better way. Your heart has a chakra that vibrates, and with the right amount of resonance, it can exude a calmness that will help you.

So, how do you meditate for the heart? What is an excellent meditation that will help with this? Good thing you're here because you're about to find out in this book!

A simple Meditation to Open the Heart

To help you open the heart, you begin with the following. Sit in a comfy position, close your eyes, and proceed to breathe in and breathe out, and as you breathe in and breathe out, let go of all the gunk that's stuck inside of you. Picture that it's a new day, a new time period, so you don't want to carry the old stuff with you.

Take one hand and put it on the heart, and then one on the belly. As you breathe, pay mind to how comfy this feels, and be aware that you can do this whenever to help take care of yourself.

At this point, you can pay note to your breathing and how it calms you, how it lets you go of yesterday, and how it gives you that feeling of safety. As you do this, realize you're here for yourself, and as you release the tensions of yesterday, let your attention come to this day. Pay attention to the hour, the time that you're in, and pay attention to your day, and how it's going to be incredible.

Keep your heart open, and picture letting the universe coming in.

Finally, finish off with some breathing in and then breathing out and slowly open your eyes.

This is a good one to first awaken the heart, and it is a great one to start the day.

Meditating to connect with the heart's energy

This is a seven-step process to help you connect with the energy from the heart, and it's both simple, yet truly effective. To begin, you sit in a position that is comfortable, and from there, close your eyes.

Let the thoughts of the outside world go, even if for a moment.

Once they are gone, focus on the spiritual heart center, which is the middle of your chest, where the heart is. Become aware that the heart is well a space and a point of awareness where feelings come in and leave. At the base of it, the heart is empty, and there are peace and subtle light. You may picture this light, whether it be white, gold, pink, or blue. don't strain though, just take in whatever is there.

At this point, put your attention on the center of the heart, and from there, breathe in a gentle manner and let the breath flow to the heart, picturing a soft, pastel light moving into the chest, where the heart is.

Next, you should let the breath go inwards and then outwards, and from there, ask your heart what it must say. don't phrase it as an order, but instead, a general statement that you want your heart to express itself.

At this point, you'll want to sit and listen for about 5-10 minutes. Listen to your heart, and it will release various emotions, wishes, fears, and memories, and there is a lot in there. You will find yourself paying attention.

If there is a strong emotion, you might feel he breath change, but experience what it is, and if you feel yourself daydream, bring the attention back to the center of the heart.

When you're done, you should thank the heart for what it says, and let the thoughts and feelings go. The feelings that come up are often repressed, and this is a way to purify the heart. It is healthy, and when you're done, open your eyes and breathe. You'll feel refreshed and better than ever before.

A second Meditation for Opening the Heart

This is a great one to help you open yourself up and build more kindness. Before you begin, you must open your heart, and that's the generalized purpose of this mediation.

To begin, you should find a place where you cannot be interrupted and give yourself time without various distractions. At this point, sit down, close your eyes, and breathe. Once you've gotten comfy, you should recall something that is challenging or difficult, whatever is causing you stress. Feel free to experience the struggle, emotional discomfort, or distress. At this point, become aware that this is a moment of discomfort and struggle, and you can acknowledge that it is stressful, haunting, painful, or you might speak the words that you feel.

You will want to recognize the struggle, stress, and what you're suffering, and realize that it's a part of life that will link you to the humanity that you have. However, don't let this overwhelm you. Remember, you're not alone and that others have struggled in the same way that you have.

At this point, put your hands on top of the heart. Take some deep breaths, relax the tension that you're holding, and when you breathe out, feel the stress as it disperses and leaves the body, along with the warm and gentle touch from the hearts that are on the chest. Feel the comforting feeling of the light building within the hands, spreading to the heart. At this point, let this energy flow from you, spreading out.

At this moment, you should ask yourself what you need to hear and feel right now in order to provide kindness to yourself. You can ask if you can be kind to yourself, forgive, be strong, be compassionate, learn to accept yourself, be patient, and give yourself the compassion that you need.

Repeat this and continue to speak this. Feel the energy start to disperse and change, and when you're done, thank your heart as you come out of this, and you'll start to realize that your heart is open, and you'll be able to put together the self-compassion that you'll need when you need it the most. This is the best way to clear away blocks, open up the heart, and feel better.

Meditation for the heart will allow you to relax and become a better person than you want to be, and it's a great way to help you improve on your own personal character and let go of the past so that you can be happier and brighter as well.

Bedtime Meditation

Short Stories Against Anxiety and Stress and Helping the Adult Fall Asleep

Denmark is high up north, where Germany stops. * There is still a king there today, but he is no longer there to govern, but usually visits kindergartens because his wife likes children so much.

But a long time ago, the Danish king was very powerful. As all kings used to do, he always wanted to increase his land so that he would become even more powerful. So he also had to conquer another country. That was not easy. In the south of Denmark was Germany, then the kingdoms of Hanover and Prussia. He could not mess with them because they had many more soldiers than he. Likewise, the Swedes, whose country lies next to Denmark.

So he looked north. Far behind the sea was Greenland. This is a huge country, but at the time, it was very little known, and it was supposed to be very cold there. So he had three ships loaded from the royal fleet. On each, he put a brave knight and several soldiers, as well as horses and all kinds of war equipment.

Then it went off to Greenland in the terribly cold north. When the ships arrived, they first saw a lot of ice and snow. The knights put on their armor and went ashore to conquer it. But no one was visible, and the knights froze in their iron armor on the ice, so they could not move. They kicked wildly, clawing their iron armor hard to free themselves from the ice.

A few of the other soldiers had to make a fire to get them released. As a result, of course, the armor on the feet was pretty hot, and the knights burned their feet. They shopped around wildly until they were finally free and quickly disappeared on the ship.

Then one tried to bring the horses ashore because one should conquer Greenland. The horses struggled hard, but after a few meters, they also got stuck in the snow. The soldiers could not walk in the high snow and froze miserably so that finally all went with their horses back on the ships, and Greenland could not conquer first. When the knights sat around thinking and pondering, the lookout on the ship's mast reported: "Enemy ahead !!"

And indeed, the knights saw in astonishment how a sleigh came with very small horses. They were astonished even more when they discovered that it was not horses but many dogs in front of a sled so effortlessly whizzing across the snow.

Everyone brought their rifles and lances and feared that they would have to defend themselves. But there was only one man on the sled, an Eskimo. He greeted them in a very friendly way and was happy to see so many people because in Greenland, not so many people live, and one is often quite lonely and alone. He welcomed everyone and asked them if they would not visit him in the evening, his wife would cook a nice soup of seal meat for them.

From whom you are greeted so friendly, you can fight badly against, and so put three of the knights on the dogsled, but without their heavy armor. Husch - you rushed over the landscape to a strange hut, which was made entirely of snow. It's called an igloo, and it's round, but it's very nice and warm!

When they had eaten, they thanked each other, and the Eskimo drove them back to their ships by dog sled. Then it was decided to drive back to Denmark.

They then reported everything to the king. He held advice with his ministers on how to conquer Greenland. They also asked a wise old man named Count Johannsen. The count whispered his suggestion in the ear of the king, and he was thrilled!

He sent his steward to the city to buy whatever vanilla powder he could get. Then he equipped a ship again, but this time the knights should put on thick fur coats and take sleds with them. In addition, the whole load compartment was full of vanilla powder!

Arrived in Greenland, they were greeted by Eskimos again; it was already known by now. The soldiers from Denmark brought a lot of fresh snow and made it with their vanilla powder from delicious vanilla ice cream. They gave it to the Eskimos.

They had never eaten anything like that! They were crazy about it and still wanted to have more. The knights, however, kept everything under wraps and first wanted to speak to the Eskimo leader, who was quickly brought for them. With him, the knights made a contract that now Greenland would belong to Denmark, and for that, the Eskimos would get as much vanilla ice cream as they could eat.

Then the knights sailed home with their ship and told their king that Greenland would now belong to Denmark, without there being a war!

And that's how it is today, so you can ask every Dane.

* Inspired by "The danish king - good night stories" - Christina Cherry.
https://christinacherry.com/the-danish-king-good-night-stories.html

Short Stories to Help Adult Improve Morale, Self-Esteem and Their Imagination

Before we begin this journey downwards into the deepest realms of our sub-conscious, let us take a minute to physically and mentally and spiritually acclimate ourselves into being with the awareness of our inner-sanctum, our internal workings.

We will begin by going to a place of comfort, ideally a bed, or a very comfortable reclining chair, and we will relax our bodies to the furthest extent possible. Now, close your eyes, staying firmly on your back, with your arms relaxed at your sides and your legs rested downwards. Take one deep breath in, through your nostrils, counting slowly to four, and one deep breath out, through your nostrils again, counting slowly to four.

Breathe in the breath of the spirit and breathe out the stress of the day. Now is the time to rest. Become aware of nothing but the air flowing through your nostrils, envision a steady flowing stream, smooth inhalations and exhalations, your body become weightier and more relaxed with each passing cycle of breath.

Allow your thoughts to become completely still, as you focus on your core, your solar plexus, allowing your thoughts to flow outwards past your vision until they escape your being, while only holding and retaining the pure awareness of spirit, the holy serenity of the mind and body.

Breathe in, one, two, three, four, then breathe out, one, two, three, four, each breath becoming slower.

One... two... three... four... One... two... three... four... One... two... three... four... One... two... three... four... One... two... three... four... One... two... three... four... One... two... three... four...

Continue this pattern of breath, expanding, and sink down deeper into yourself, becoming a voyeur of your own still, relaxed body, lost in time.

Become lost in this experience as you journey further into the trance, and prepare for the road we are about to embark upon. Draw further and further away from your still, lying body, and into the realm of imagination, where images grow, the land of dreams that you are about to become one with. Erase your mind of all that is within it currently, and prepare the landscape for a new and fresh experience, in the farther reaches of reality.

One... two... three... four... inhale... One... two... three... four... exhale... One... two... three... four... inhale...

One... two... three... four... exhale...

Now, with your mind, body, and spirit rested totally, entranced, and fertile, let us begin.

It is nighttime; it seems like it has been forever. You are in the backseat of a car with a blanket, and you are very, very comfortable. The car vibrates softly on the road. It seems to be going at a good and consistent speed. Every once in a while, it will rock itself to a top, sweetly, then hum back along until it reaches another steady speed for a good long while. Who is driving?

You don't know.

You see the back of his head. It is a warm, friendly-looking man. He is calm and still and has his eyes on the road.

Where are you going?

You don't remember.

You had some destination in mind. It occurs to you. You are in a taxi, a taxi that was called for you. Wherever you are going, you know it is a safe destination, and where you are meant to be.

However long it takes for you to get there, you will be comfortable, and you will be safe, and, you feel, the longer it takes, the better, because here, where you are now, is some kind of paradise, totally calm, and safe, and secure, and still, and alone, in this backseat.

If you were to look up in the rearview mirror of the front seat, you would see the driver notice your gaze and match it, and give a warm, affectionate smile, then avert his eyes back to the road.

There is no nervous, idle chitchat in this peaceful environment.

There is an unspoken bond between you and the driver, a bond of the heart, and you both are so comfortable with each other you might as well not even be separate beings. He knows where you are going, and he is taking you there, and you are as safe in his hands as you would be on your own, so it is now allowed for you to totally relax and pay absolutely no mind to anything.

There is nothing else. Whatever worries existed in life outside of this taxi, they are neither here nor there.

You are going to your destination, and on this long, safe trip through eternal night, you have absolutely nothing to worry about that has not already been taken care of. You do not have a seatbelt on, because that is how safe you are.

You are lying back against the right backseat door, with a very comfortable pillow, cuddled up in the world's fluffiest, richest, warmest blanket. It seems as if it is very cold outside the taxi, maybe even a little chilly inside of it, as you can feel on your face, the only exposed skin outside of the blanket.

You can see the frost and condensation on the windows of the taxi, slow drips of frosty water going from the top to the bottom, slightly curved back by the momentum of the moving vehicle, then many more taking their place.

There might even be a light hint of snow, few and far between flakes dusting down and providing a light accouterment to the pitch-blackness of the sky, but you are so drowsy and so relaxed, you don't even bother to tell for sure. No buildings are present from the low angle you see out the window, all though there might be many slightly below, but you do see the occasional calming orange glow of a streetlight. And beyond these gothic lanterns, your attention is drawn to the infinite array of stars.

There are more stars than you have ever seen, big and small, bright and beautiful, yet so very, very far away. Just, to you, now, a calm reminder of life far away from this planet, from yourself, life going on and on; infinity. Far away from you, you begin to make out the static sounds of what might be a highway, the low buzzing drone of many, many cars going many, many places, so far away, so apart from you.

It is incredibly soothing, like some low and consistent heartbeat of the world. You are just one traveler, in the veins, going where you are going, and it feels so peaceful to you to just become that one part in a sea of infinite parts, doing what you are doing, being who you are, simply existing, as the world exists around you.

The infinite night, the constant wee hours of the morning, you zoned out a long time ago into this peaceful, blissful state, and you aren't really sure how long you have been in the backseat of this taxi since you even noticed that you were. And if that were to be defined, then how long before that.

It seems circular like you might have just been a passenger in the backseat of this taxi, nestled up in this blanket, protected from the elements, warm, but so alive, forever. For all you know, this could just be life; calm, quiet, consistent, relaxed, for eternity. You lose focus on any one particular thing, and, though your eyes are still open, you don't really know what you are looking at; just blackness, the pitch-blackness of this eternal night, where you are a passenger.

The hum of the heartbeat of the world takes over, and your body relaxes into a state in which you begin to leave it and become everyone and everything, everywhere, going wherever. Somewhere, sometime, the taxi driver flips on the warm signal of the radio, AM, and it is just one more beautiful layer of white noise atop the infinite.

You hear, somewhere, voices talking, and music existing upon music in the backgrounds of our souls.

In this warm cocoon, the infinite layers of life dance into oblivion all around you, and you are succumbed, in glorious awe, totally relaxed, and tranquil, and entranced in its hypnotic beauty. Lifetimes must pass, as they always do, in this backseat, with you as a passenger going somewhere, anywhere, to your destination.

The heartbeat of the world and the hum of the radio and the steady, consistent, non-stop calm rumble of the taxi on your whole body begin to become one sensation, the buzzing of the world soul, the eternal drone.

You are what you are, going where you are going, and you become this, and all that you are drifts away, and there is nothing, and you are asleep.

Conclusion

We've all heard that reflection prompts more prominent mental lucidity, lower levels of pressure, and diminished uneasiness. Yet, how does contemplation advantage the mind? Studies have demonstrated that care practice achieves positive physiological changes that make the association among contemplation, and the cerebrum considerably progressively significant.

In ongoing decades, contemplation has turned out to be progressively ordinary. Individuals are investing energy in working with their brains, following their breath, and figuring out how to welcome the intensity of the present minute. Reflection gatherings are springing up all over – in schools, networks, senior focuses, and past. It's moved toward becoming so standard that even the business network has joined the development is fixated on reflection, and there's new proof it improves the mind.

Research in the field of brain science has affirmed what each meditator knows: reflection is useful for body and soul. Science is currently ready to strengthen the cases by demonstrating how contemplation physically impacts the remarkably unpredictable organ between our ears. Ongoing logical proof affirms that reflection sustains the pieces of the cerebrum that add to prosperity. Moreover, it appears that a customary practice deprive the pressure and uneasiness related pieces of the cerebrum of their sustenance.

Stress is one of the most weakening emotions we can have. Stress is a psychological approach that teaches people the skills they need to cope with anxiety and stress. Not only mental stress, but also many cases that can lead to physical health problems, both short and long term.

One sad thing about stress is often not as stressful as stress itself, although it is very unpleasant for the person to get stressed, but the fear of the reaction of others if they want to have confidence in a friend, family, or co-worker, even professionals of stress management.

At an equal time, we all realize the effects that pressure can have, and in case you examine this book in search of a treatment or at least an alleviation from personal pressure or a cherished one, the effects of strain need no similar explanation.

As you have got learned, stress control begins by figuring out the assets of stress for your existence. It isn't as easy as it looks. The actual assets of your strain are not usually obvious, and it's far very smooth to ignore your thoughts, emotions, and strain behaviors.

Another sad fact about stress management, and being a stress and anger management specialist myself, and I know it very well, is the widespread belief that stress management doesn't matter.

That is a "spongy" concept that is not necessary, or only for the weak.

Stress management is very important and overcome anxiety is crucial for success at work and for a healthy life.

Sometimes, life can be a very stressful event. We all go through moments where we feel that our anxiety and depression is going to swallow us whole. If you have ever felt this way, just realize that you are not alone in feeling this way.

Even if this is your first encounter with meditation, I hope that this little book has hooked you on this fascinating and never ending world.

To your success!